The Art and Science of Dealing with Toxic People and Relationships

The Practical Manual for Handling a Narcissistic Wife, Husband, or Parent, and Leading a Happier and Productive Life

I0531773

Richard Banks

Thank You!

Thank you for your purchase.

I am dedicated to making the most enriching and informational content. I hope it meets your expectations and you gain a lot from it.

Your comments and feedback are important to me because they help me to provide the best material possible. So, if you have any questions or concerns, please email me at richardbanks.books@gmail.com.

Again, thank you for your purchase.

INTRODUCTION

Congratulations on purchasing *How to Deal with Toxic People and Relationships,* and thank you for doing so.

"You can't go back and change the beginning, but you can start where you are and change the ending."
- C. S. Lewis

Before anything else, I want you to read the above quotation as a way to understand why you have this book in your hands. It's important to read every chapter so you know how to identify, deal with, and, most of all, remove toxic people and relationships from your life so you can begin to lead a life of positivity, love, and freedom.

Humans are social animals. We're born, we mature, and we eventually succumb to death. But in this seemingly simple cycle, there are numerous complex paths and struggles that we must experience to make it to the other end. As it's nearly impossible for us to isolate ourselves and pursue our spiritual path unaligned and unentangled with others, we tend to search for connection and growth through the relationships we form with others during our lifetime. Every relationship we have—be it with our parents, siblings, friends, or romantic partners—influences and shapes the kind of person we are and our mental, emotional, physical, and spiritual well-being. Therefore, it's important to pay attention to the kind of people we share the table with and keep an eye out for people who are toxic to us. We must take the necessary actions to ensure we don't let them negatively affect us with their toxicity.

Dealing with toxic people can be extremely difficult, especially if the toxic person in question is a parent, daughter, son, husband, or wife. In such a case, you must remember that not all toxic people intend to be toxic. Most fail to recognize their actions as harmful to those in their vicinity. Toxic people are often struggling with their traumas and other underlying emotional disturbances, which makes them engage in toxic behaviors. Although this can, in no way, be used as an excuse, it does help to understand that their actions aren't solely directed at us but are more a reflection of their inner mental and emotional state. In a situation where the toxic person in question is someone you love dearly and care about, if their behavior and actions remain unchanged—even after multiple confrontations about how they make you feel—you have to realize that it's time to cut this person out of your life.

With the help of this book, I hope you find strength in the knowledge that life after a toxic person is difficult at first but gets happier with every passing day. You may be able to recognize toxic patterns and people in your life and know exactly when it's time to cut them off, but you avoid doing so because you're not sure if you're making the right decision. If this is the case, this book will help you, too. In this book, I go into the details of identifying toxic relationships and understanding what makes a relationship toxic. You'll learn how you can deal with difficult people in a way that makes you feel more confident. This involves developing healthier communication skills, building intrapersonal boundaries, finding forgiveness for yourself and others, and managing complex emotions. Through this book, you'll also learn what a healthy relationship looks like and how you can make your existing relationships healthier by incorporating particular engagement patterns and behaviors. By the end of this book, you'll know how to cut your toxic cords to people, beliefs, addictions, and places—which is essential if you want to lead a healthier and happier life and discover your true purpose in life.

You may be wondering, "Why go through all the trouble of eliminating someone from my life if I'm able to keep dealing with them?" That's a valid question. And I'll give you a simple answer—to save yourself the repercussions of what happens if you don't. What do you think makes a person toxic? Emotional turmoil and unprocessed trauma can make a person experiencing these things bitter. And, naturally, a bitter person will make others feel pain because of their hurtful actions and words. You may have heard the saying, "hurt people hurt people." That's true of toxic people as well. If you're dealing with a toxic person daily, there's a good chance you'll develop some toxic traits yourself as a coping mechanism. Although this may seem helpful at first, you'll notice that you pick up more traits over time as long as you continue to interact with a person who's adamant about remaining toxic. It's worth taking the trouble to cut a toxic person out of your life if they're unwilling to change because, sooner or later, they'll turn you into a version of yourself you'll neither recognize nor like. In a circumstance where you can't cut off contact with this person, it would be wise to limit your time with them so their toxic traits don't affect you in a way you don't want them to.

If you're currently experiencing a toxic relationship and don't know what to do about it, this book may be just what you need. I've tried my best to not only provide you with the knowledge you need to deal with toxic situations and people but also to motivate you to make the necessary positive changes in your life. All you need to do is put the knowledge provided in this book into action. If you read this entire book and memorize every guideline but don't put the knowledge into practice, it won't be of any benefit to you. The life you dream of having may seem out of reach at this moment, but I'd ask you have to have faith in yourself and remind yourself of the power you hold.

Toxic people may make you feel like you cannot achieve what you want in life. I urge you to stop looking at yourself through the eyes of a toxic person and look deeper into your capabilities and talents. You'll realize that what you need to achieve your dream life you already have within yourself. Finally, I'd like to wish you the very best and remind you that it's time for you to take back your power from the clutches of the toxic people in your life and show them just how powerful you truly are.

There are plenty of books on this subject on the market; thanks again for choosing this one! Every effort was made to ensure it's full of as much helpful information as possible. Please enjoy!

CHAPTER 1: TOXIC AND NARCISSISTIC BEHAVIOR

In this chapter, I'll give you a sound understanding of toxic and narcissistic behavior. By the time you reach the end of it, you'll know exactly what you're dealing with. You'll also have the courage to take the necessary actions to save yourself from situations in which you must interact with a toxic or narcissistic person. Toxicity and narcissism are intense, hostile behaviors that no one should be dealing with. They can cause severe damage to your mental and physical health and peace of mind. The moment you understand this is what you're dealing with, you shouldn't waste time. You must take action. I'm sure you have every intention of doing so. That's why you bought this book. So, without further ado, let me get into the details.

Toxic Behavior

Recognizing a toxic person is more about identifying how they make you feel rather than what they do or say. Being able to spot their harmful behavior is the first step to minimizing their impact. Another equally important thing to keep in mind is that many toxic people don't intend to be so. Their emotions unconsciously bring out a side of them that they might not even be aware of. Therefore, it's on you to notice your reactions to their words or behavior rather than trying to analyze what they're doing. You'll have greater control over your feelings and actions when you know better ways to deal with these people—no matter what kind of situation you come across.

Warning Signs

There are both external and internal warning signs of toxic people and relationships, and it falls on you to be aware of these so you can be a better judge of character and identify the toxic people in your life.

- ### *Internal Warning Signs*

  Internal warning signs refer to being aware of how you feel when dealing with a toxic person. Toxic traits aren't always physical or verbal. Most of the time, it's your own emotions that you should focus on. Why? Because even though these signs aren't so evident to the eyes, they tend to have even more impact. Here are the six key internal warning signs to look out for:

  o **You feel like you're being manipulated into something you don't want to do -** Have you felt like you were being manipulated into doing something you didn't want to do? If you have, know for a fact that no matter who the other person is and what position they have in your life, no one should ever force you to do anything against your wishes or will. If there's something you aren't comfortable with, the other person should respect those boundaries and those decisions. A toxic person might not even realize that they're doing this, but if you feel you're being forced, step back.

o **You're constantly confused by the person's behavior** - A toxic person will always confuse you with their behavior because they aren't completely aware of what they want. They're often cynical people who find fault in everything you do. Naturally, they'll interact with you in different ways at different points in time. This can be troublesome because a lot can depend on the emotional balance you have with other people in your life.

o **You feel like you deserve an apology that never comes** - With toxic people, there will be instances in which they act or behave in a way that's insulting or hurtful. But this kind of person rarely apologizes for anything they say or anything that goes wrong simply because they aren't ready to accept what they've done. It's either intentional—where their vanity makes them incapable of apologizing—or unintentional—where they don't consider what impact their behavior might have on others. Any rational person should have the ability to understand when they're hurting others. If they don't, that's a problem.

o **You feel you must always defend yourself when you're with this person** - A common characteristic of every toxic person is playing the victim and trying to put the blame on others. As a result, you have to continuously defend yourself when interacting with them. You might not have done anything at all, but because they have an escapist mentality, they'll try their best to twist the truth and put all the blame on you to save face.

o **You never feel entirely comfortable around them** - No matter how close you are to this person, if they're inherently toxic, and you start realizing it, you'll no longer feel comfortable around them. This could be for several reasons. Firstly, a toxic person gives off negative energy, which antagonizes you over time. Secondly, you look to relationships for empathy, consistency, and trust, and when you don't get these, it's not possible for you to feel comfortable.

o **You feel insecure and inadequate in their presence** - Toxic people will invariably make you feel bad about yourself. Even if the topic of discussion is about something positive, they'll make sure to turn it in a way that makes you feel something is lacking in you and, if anything goes wrong, you're the reason. It becomes more about what you're doing wrong and them pointing that out all the time. If this continues, there may come a point where you fail to see anything good in yourself or around you.

• **External Warning Signs**

Unlike the internal warning signs—which are based on how you feel around toxic people— external signs are visible in a person's words and behavior. These signs highlight their toxicity and are based on how they treat you and others around them. Here are the six key external warning signs to look out for:

o **Inconsistency** - They tend to be inconsistent because they lack empathy and genuinely don't care about what others might go through because of their actions. Let's say this particular person in your life tends to always get what they want. They'll do this with no regard for how much moral strain it puts on you. They'll never be on time or do what they say they will simply because your needs aren't important to them. Be aware of people who have it in their nature to be inconsistent and who do it without any remorse.

o **They always need your attention** - Toxic people always need your attention. They're never happy with how much they receive from you, and they always need more. They want everyone around them to be at their service, and their inherent feeling of inadequacy makes them want others to give them more attention because they crave constant validation.

o **They're always starting drama** - With toxic people, there's an endless strain of drama. This kind of person can't do anything without being dramatic about it simply because, for them, it's all about themselves and their entertainment. Either they'll victimize themselves or mistreat others. They'll make up stories to mislead others or do something that can bring harm to others' lives.

o **They don't respect your boundaries** - This is because they lack empathy. You or anyone else in their life is just a means to get what they want. In that regard, whether that oversteps your boundaries is none of their concern.

o **They manipulate you to get what they want** - Manipulation is second nature to toxic people, and they're unapologetic about it. They're quite aware of what they're doing, and they use it to their advantage to get what they want.

o **They have substance abuse problems** - Addiction and toxic relationships are often linked, with substance abuse co-occurring with intimate-partner abuse in 40 to 60% of cases. However, it can extend to other relationships as well. In toxic relationships, the abuser often uses substances to cope with their own painful experiences, contributing to increased mistreatment of others and possibly abuse.

Now that I've established the warning signs of toxic people, let me take you through some of the reasons why people become toxic.

Why Are Some People So Toxic?

A toxic person is anyone whose behavior adds negativity or stress to your life. We often find ourselves asking, "Why is this person behaving this way?" or, "What led this person to be so antagonistic?"

Psychotherapist and life coach Jodie Gole says this about toxic people: "Often the person is deeply wounded, and for whatever reason, they are not yet able to take responsibility for their wounding, their feelings, their needs and their subsequent problems in life." So, it's not that these people are inherently toxic – they're wounded. But the way they unconsciously act out their wounding toward others can be labeled 'toxic' because this behavior can be hurtful and damaging.

Toxic people feel an unconscious need to bring others down to boost their own feelings of self-worth. They're usually completely unaware of their unconscious need to hurt others and ignorant of the fact that they do that because they don't feel good about themselves. They'll find ways to bring others down – intentionally or unintentionally – because it feels like the only way they can lift themselves up. And the effects on those around them can be damaging. Some of these people go to extraordinary lengths to hurt others as a way to make themselves feel better, which can be really painful if this person is a family member or friend.

Toxicity in people isn't considered a mental disorder. But there could be underlying mental problems that cause someone to act in toxic ways, including a personality disorder, post-traumatic stress disorder, or bipolar disorder. As author Christian Baloga said: "Pay no attention to toxic words. What people say is often a reflection of themselves, not you."

Narcissism

Now, let's take a deeper dive into the concept of narcissism by discussing what narcissism is, how to identify narcissistic people, the types of narcissism, and its traits.

What Is Narcissism?

In simple terms, narcissism is a psychological condition in which a person has an inflated sense of self—so much so that they fail to look beyond themselves at all. They have an intense superiority complex that makes them high-handed and downright rude.

Narcissists' inflated sense of self makes them think they're better than everyone. They're entitled people who tend to lack empathy, and they need admiration because they truly believe they deserve it. They're extremely toxic and can cause a great deal of psychological and physical harm to the people around them.

How Do People Become Narcissistic?

There are three main reasons why people develop narcissism. The first is the environment they grow up in. Our surroundings and upbringing have a lot to do with how our brain develops and functions. When a kid grows up in a toxic environment within a disturbed family, or when they aren't taught healthy values and are made to face either extreme criticism or extreme leniency, it's natural for them to grow up to be narcissists. The second reason is the genetics of the person. Narcissism can be inherent, wherein the child inherits this trait from a parent or other ancestor. The third reason is neurobiological. A child could have had a normal upbringing but still develop narcissism simply because of the way their brain starts perceiving and reacting to things over time.

Character Traits of Narcissistic People

Narcissistic people can be recognized by certain common traits, some of which I'll mention here. I'm sure that after you read this, you'll be able to recognize a narcissist easier and more quickly. Narcissists have an exaggerated sense of self. If they're in business, they demand admiration and appreciation from everyone around them. Narcissists are superficial in all types of relationships because of their lack of a sense of empathy. Everything begins and ends with them. They have a high level of identity disturbance because of their inherent superiority complex, so they fail to attach themselves emotionally to anyone. As a result, they lose their sense of self to a large extent. Narcissists can become self-destructive because they become bored easily with anything that's not about them. They rarely have genuine friends and, therefore, are lonely. They tend to become vulnerable in their current situation because they can't handle failure of any kind.

There are always reasons behind why people behave a certain way. We'll now explore some of the reasons why narcissists behave as they do.

Why Do Narcissists Behave the Way They Do?

As I've already mentioned, narcissists behave the way they do because they're insecure and have an extremely fragile sense of self. They've been wounded in the past and have never been able to recover. People who find it difficult to be in their own skin will naturally turn to the world for validation and admiration. They try to hide that sense of insecurity under the guise of toughness, ill behavior, and, of course, a pretentious superiority complex. No person is inherently bad, and proper therapy will discover the reasons for a narcissist's toxicity.

What's more unfortunate for narcissists, however, is that, in the process of hiding their low self-esteem while trying to gain admiration from others, their actions tend to turn everyone around them against them in the long run. Their actions thus have the complete opposite effect of what they want to achieve. Instead of being admired, they end up being disliked and avoided. This, in turn, stimulates their need for more admiration and validation.

Narcissism and toxicity correlate strongly with

28

superiority and inferiority complexes. Let's explore this relationship further.

Superiority Complex vs. Inferiority Complex

A superiority complex is when a person projects an inflated sense of themselves while trying to hide fears of failure and inferiority as well as their true feelings. On the other hand, an inferiority complex refers to an actual or a perceived sense of lack or inability that makes a person feel bad about themselves, which can lead to aggression and other toxic behaviors. Living with either of these complexes isn't good for anyone due to the accumulation of toxic traits that are inherent in each of them.

Narcissists already suffer from a superiority complex for the reasons stated above. They also try to take advantage of people who are meek or have an inferiority complex. However, oddly enough, one of the root causes of narcissism can also be an inherent sense of inferiority that forces them to manifest

29

toughness and apparent superiority. Someone with a superiority complex will never take into consideration what others think or have to say. In contrast, a person who suffers from an inferiority complex will be all about soliciting the opinions of others because they don't have the confidence to take action based on their own thoughts and decisions alone. In both of these complexes, the people around them suffer because they need to tackle all the issues that come with them.

When you compare these two complexes, of course, you'll find many descriptions of how they're different and what causes each of them, along with many suggestions for how you can deal with people who have one of these complexes. What they have in common is, first, they're both toxic. For the person afflicted and those around them, these complexes can cause severe damage. Feeling either superior or inferior can motivate a person to take steps that are impractical or even self-destructive. Secondly, narcissism is strongly linked to both of these complexes. One can be considered the root cause of narcissism, and the other is a defense mechanism that narcissists use to cope.

Can Toxic People Change?

So far, we've talked at length about the reasons why people are difficult and toxic and how you can recognize them. I'm sure several such people have already come to mind who fall under these categories. The question that naturally arises now is whether such people can change. The answer is, yes, they can change but only to a certain extent. How much they can change, or the extent of their progress depends on the individual. The person needs to first realize they're toxic and want to change before any change is possible.

Toxic people need to acknowledge their behavior and be open to accepting help, be it in the form of psychotherapy or a genuine conversation with a trusted friend. It's unrealistic to think this change will happen overnight. That isn't possible. It depends a lot on their environment and the willingness of people close to them to help them on their journey to change. They'll require genuine help, and those around them should be ready to provide that help. Unless that's there, the toxic behavior will continue.

People who display toxic behavior must realize they don't need to pretend to be something they're not and are free to express how they feel. They need to feel safe in exposing their vulnerabilities. If this kind of support is established, toxic people can change. If the toxicity is assumed to be genetic, it could be more challenging for them to change after all this time. That being said, we should never lose hope.

I hope this chapter has been informative and provided you with some of the answers you were looking for. Now that you're able to better recognize toxic and narcissistic people, I'm sure it will be easier for you to find ways of handling them and protecting yourself.

Chapter 2: Relationships – The Good, The Bad, and The Ugly

In this chapter, I'll be talking about nuances of relationships that will help you understand the various shades that a relationship goes through and what should be tolerated and what shouldn't. You often say yes to something your partner asks you to do even when you aren't comfortable with it. You might think that because your partner asks for something, it's necessary to agree to it because, after all, this is a person with whom you're in a relationship. It could be something psychological or something physical and materialistic. They might ask you to do something, or they might practice a certain kind of behavior that you aren't okay with. Know this for a fact: You don't have to say yes just because you're in a relationship. You're an equal partner in that relationship, as is the other person. Only those things should be done that are okay with both people involved.

Relationships are tricky to begin with, and let no one tell you otherwise. No matter how mature both you and your partner are, you're still two unique people who had different upbringings and different past experiences. You've both decided to share your time, but that doesn't mean things will start aligning magically. It takes a lot of effort from both parties to see to it that nothing happens to make either partner feel uncomfortable or unsafe. However, there will inevitably be problems when one or both partners have toxic traits.

As I've mentioned in the previous chapter, some people are toxic by nature, and they're conscious of it. In contrast, some people engage in toxic behavior unconsciously and don't know that what they're doing is causing problems for other people. Though it isn't on you to tag someone as good or bad, you nonetheless must communicate what you're not comfortable with and what makes you uneasy. If your partner is reasonable, they'll realize their mistake and cease saying or doing that thing. But if you find you're barking up the wrong tree—that is, things aren't changing for the better even after you point out the effects of their behavior to them—that's your cue to disengage from that relationship. It might seem like a drastic step when I say it like that, but I think, by the end of this chapter, you'll see why I feel so strongly about this.

Introduction to Relationships

Understanding what a healthy relationship looks like will help you better identify a toxic one. You'll then realize what should be expected and what should never happen. I'll now talk about certain aspects of relationships that will give you a better grasp of things.

Why Are Relationships So Difficult?

Let me assure you that you aren't the only one who finds relationships difficult. So, don't ever make the mistake of beating yourself up about it. We've all been brought up on movies and storybooks that rarely show

35

us the real picture. Our parents also made it a point to keep their problems from us as much as possible when we were growing up so our psyche wasn't affected in the wrong way. While it wasn't wrong on their part to want us to grow up in a peaceful environment, problems arise if we grow up thinking that a romantic relationship will be all hearts and flowers. When we enter a relationship, our illusions start crashing down, and we realize it's not what we envisioned. Let's explore some reasons for this.

- **Having expectations can be brutal –** Despite what your common sense may tell you, research shows that people are surprisingly inept at predicting how they'll feel in various situations. For example, one study found that newlywed couples tended to estimate that their happiness levels would rise (or at least stay the same) over the first four years after marriage. In reality, their levels of happiness tended to diminish over that period. It's physically and psychologically impossible to agree to every request—no matter how small or large—that your partner makes of you. The sooner we realize that, the better. But the problem is, not everyone is good at taking "no" for an answer. The heartbreak that comes with recognizing we have unrealistic expectations is tough to deal with.

- **Intimacy isn't easy** – You might have gone into a relationship thinking you're ready to be open and vulnerable. But guess what. Intimacy is complex, and not everyone is okay with it. No one will know for sure what they are and aren't comfortable with until they're faced with it, right? When you or your partner realize you're having issues with intimacy or certain aspects of it, it's vital to figure out how to address this! If the other person is genuine and open, they'll cooperate, and both of you can find a way out. However, if they're toxic, solving the problem won't even matter to them, leaving you in an unhealthy space physically and mentally.

- **Romance isn't constant or consistent** – It's in those instances where romance or commitment is lacking that we get the sudden feeling of not knowing a person to whom we thought we'd grown close. You can look at them and see a stranger once their mask comes off. You shouldn't have to wonder which version of someone you're going to get from one day to the next. If you're on pins and needles waiting to see what kind of mood someone will be in every day, that's unfair to you and unhealthy. Yes, romance is imperative for most relationships to work, but it's only one of the many other things needed for two people to stay together. What's important to understand is that the romance will start fading unless you both are on the same page in your understanding of what makes a good relationship.

- **Managing conflicts can be stressful–** Managing conflicts is a must for any relationship to work. Your relationship will indeed have conflicts because that's a natural part of interacting with almost anyone. People need to communicate for any relationship to work. One should never have a negative attitude toward solving problems, believing it's a difficult task. Yes, it may be difficult, but no one is going to solve those problems for you. Addressing conflicts has to be viewed as necessary and meaningful by both parties. The attitude should be to want to solve conflicts because, at the end of the day, that relationship is strong enough to endure the misunderstandings and resentment that will follow if those conflicts aren't managed well. When either or both partners aren't up for solving conflicts and communicating, it can be tough to maintain a healthy relationship.

Now that we've established some potential problems, let's see how a healthy partnership works.

What Do Healthy Relationships Look Like?

A healthy relationship and healthy intimacy aren't utopian concepts. I agree that the time we live in shows us how problematic people, in general, and relationships, in particular, can be. However, if the people involved are honest and not afraid to be vulnerable, a healthy relationship and genuine intimacy can become a source of joy and peace for both of them.

Below are four key factors that are a must for maintaining a healthy relationship and intimacy. Keep in mind that these are pretty much true for everyone. When any of these are lacking, there will be problems, highlighting that you may be involved in a toxic relationship.

- **Consent** – Probably the most important thing to make any relationship work is consent. No matter what kind of a relationship you're in, unless both the parties say yes in their wish to do a particular thing, it shouldn't be done. It could be as small as having Chinese for dinner instead of Italian, or it could be something as significant as deciding to move in together or have a baby. Every decision that a couple makes should have a consensual agreement. The same goes for intimacy. One should never cross boundaries and be unwilling to take no for an answer.

- **Communication** – Communication is the key to having a healthy relationship. The same goes for intimacy. Especially in bed or during other intimate moments, make sure you and your partner are on the same page regarding what you have in mind through proper communication. Only then will there be no anxiety, no misunderstandings, and no needless mistakes.

- **Boundaries** – All of us have boundaries, and they should always be respected. Understanding that every person—whether this is your partner or someone else—has unique boundaries and honoring those shows them the respect they deserve as human beings. If your partner doesn't respect your boundaries and tries to physically and emotionally manipulate you to say yes to what they want, know for a fact that they're toxic and simply using you for their needs. If they genuinely care about you—as a person and as their partner—they'll respect your boundaries. The same must be true for you.

- **Trust** – A healthy relationship is based on trust. It often happens that the person you choose to be with is different from you and might have many faults, but you still decide to be with them because you trust them. You trust them with your thoughts and with your body. A relationship can only stay healthy when both partners trust each other with their insecurities and vulnerabilities. To even suspect you can't trust your partner is reason enough to not be with them. Trust is non-negotiable and should never be jeopardized.

Relationship Disorders

Relationships are hard, to say the least. A huge part of understanding healthy relationships depends on knowing how to tackle unhealthy ones that can threaten to disturb your emotional balance. It takes a lot on the part of both parties to make it work, and it's necessary to understand the nuances of human psychology that are at play here. I'll now talk about some of these nuances.

- **Codependency** - "A codependent relationship is a kind of dysfunctional relationship where one person is a caretaker and the other person takes advantage" (*9 Warning Signs of a Codependent Relationship*, 2021).

In such a relationship, one partner always has more physical and emotional responsibility while the other partner tends to do little or nothing to contribute to the health of the relationship. A codependent relationship is extremely toxic and taxing for the more responsible partner. It's often rife with problems because there's no equality between the commitment of the partners. In comparison, an interdependent relationship assures that both parties are equally responsible and invested in the whole process. It's more about helping and understanding each other while also giving them space.

- **Insecure Attachment**– A fear of abandonment and struggling to ask for help might seem like two isolated character traits, but they share one common thread. Most people who identify with these behaviors have the same attachment style, characterized by insecurity, called insecure attachment style. People with an insecure attachment style generally have trouble making emotional connections with others. They can be aggressive or unpredictable toward their loved ones—a behavior that is rooted in the lack of consistent love and affection they experienced in their childhood.

- **Interpersonal neurobiology** – Dr. Daniel Seigel has said, "We are who we are, as we are, in relation to one another." He says in his book, *"The Developing Mind, The Healing Power Of Emotion,"* that "identity is not contained so much within an individual but between individuals" (Caddell, 2020). This means we tend to become like the people we spend the most time with. People in relationships often take on each other's habits or characteristics. So, if your partner has toxic traits, it's natural that eventually you'll not only be affected by those but also may start to express them yourself.

- **Exploring core beliefs** – Relationships are challenging because not everyone grows up with the same core beliefs. It's sometimes easier for two people to stay together if they have similar core beliefs. Problems can occur when one partner's mindset and view of the world and the environment around them are completely different than the other person's. It then becomes difficult to remain on the same page about anything.

- **Shame, vulnerability, and fear** – If you're in a relationship with a toxic person, instead of helping you feel safe with your vulnerabilities and being by your side in times of need, they'll do the complete opposite. They'll make you feel ashamed in front of others, and they might even do things that make you afraid to be with them. What's more, they'll try to make you believe it's your fault to feel any of these things.

- **Intimacy disorders** – A relationship can become really difficult to handle and toxic when one or both partners have an intimacy disorder, which means they feel unsafe, uncomfortable, and reluctant to become intimate with the other person. This could be physical as well as emotional intimacy. Whatever else, a healthy relationship requires intimacy. When that's absent, it won't be as healthy as is ideal.

Attachment Theory

Attachment theory in psychology originates with the seminal work of John Bowlby (1958). Attachment theory is focused on the relationships and bonds between people, particularly long-term relationships, including those between a parent and child and between romantic partners.

According to researchers Hazan and Shaver (1987), the emotional bond that develops between adult romantic partners is partly a function of the same motivational system that gives rise to the emotional bond between infants and their caregivers. Hazan and Shaver noted that the relationship between infants and caregivers and the relationship between adult romantic partners share the following features:

• Both feel safe when the other is nearby and responsive.

• Both engage in close, intimate, bodily contact.

• Both feel insecure when the other is inaccessible.

• Both share discoveries with one another.

• Both exhibit a mutual fascination and preoccupation with one another.

• Both engage in "baby talk."

Based on these parallels, the theory concludes that the human tendency of an individual is to seek closeness and feel more secure when in the presence of the person to whom they're attached.

Four Common "Attachment Styles"

Attachment styles are expectations people develop about relationships with others. A person's attachment style is their specific way of relating to others in relationships. Here are the four most common attachment styles:

- **Secure** – There are people in relationships whose attachment to each other is based on security. They can maintain a healthy relationship because they trust each other and are secure in the relationship as well as in their personal lives. They may deal with problems that come their way individually, but, at the same time, they don't mistrust the other person. This is great for keeping misunderstandings at bay. A secure attachment is a sign of a healthy and non-toxic relationship. In this type of partnership, both partners only add positivity to the other person's life. This type of attachment isn't based on unnecessary expectations that are impossible to meet. It's based on mutual trust, allowing each other to have the needed personal space, and provides a general sense of security.

- **Anxious** – This insecure attachment style is marked by a deep fear of abandonment and insecurity. Anxiously attached people tend to be very insecure about their relationships, often worrying that their partner will leave them and thus are always hungry for validation. People with this attachment style crave emotional intimacy, even when their partner isn't ready or the situation doesn't call for it.

- **Avoidant** – Adults with an avoidant or dismissive attachment style are the opposite of those who are anxious-attached. Instead of craving intimacy, they're so wary of closeness that they try to avoid emotional connection with others. They'd prefer not to rely on others or have others rely on them. People who have an avoidant attachment style find it uncomfortable to get too emotionally close to others or to trust them fully.

- **Disorganized** – A person with this attachment style is disorganized and confused. They essentially have both the avoidant and the anxious styles combined—wanting emotional closeness and also pushing it away. They're fearful of fully trusting others, yet they need approval or validation. They often deny their feelings or are reluctant to express them. They're reluctant to develop a close romantic relationship, yet they have a dire need to feel loved by others.

How to Create Secure Attachments in Your Relationships

There are certain ideas everyone should remember before establishing any attachment to others. What should be clear in your mind are the following:

- **Take care of yourself** –_The first thing for you to realize is that unless you have a healthy relationship with yourself—with your mind and body—you won't be able to have one with anyone else. You need to be at peace to be the best companion to your partner. If you don't take care of your mind and body, it isn't possible to invest yourself in anything else successfully.

- **Team up with your partner** – Understand that your partner is a human being just like you. They're not a magician. They can't be good at everything. So, extend your genuine help and team up with them to make the relationship work. It's always a two-way journey, and unless you do your part, that ship won't sail.

- **Be there to give support at vulnerable moments** – Your partner needs to feel safe and comfortable around you, even during moments when they're vulnerable or weak. You need to make them realize through your words and actions that you'll be there not only during the good times but also the bad ones.

- **Increase your emotional intelligence -** Emotional intelligence is the ability to understand, use, and manage your own emotions in positive ways to empathize with your partner, communicate more effectively, and deal with conflict in a healthier way. Building emotional intelligence can help strengthen a romantic relationship. By understanding your emotions and how to control them, you'll better express your needs and feelings to your partner and also have more insight into how they're feeling.

- **Don't be afraid to seek therapy** - Therapy is helpful for both individuals and couples. A quality therapist will help you discover your attachment style, establish appropriate boundaries, and promote a healthy relationship.

A relationship is like a boat that you and your partner sail together on the ocean of life. Both of you might be under-prepared for the storms ahead, but when there's mutual respect, trust, and love, you both can learn how to navigate even the roughest waters. However, if you both become too busy to think about what could be better or what's wrong, even the smallest waves can be enough to turn the boat upside down. So, there will be good, bad, and ugly in every relationship, but that's how life is. If your partner is willing, grab every opportunity to help the relationship grow. If your partner isn't fully engaged in making the two of you better—together and individually—you may be in a toxic relationship. In the next chapter, we'll explore how to identify toxic relationships.

CHAPTER 3: IDENTIFYING TOXIC RELATIONSHIPS

Now that you've reached this chapter, you're likely looking for answers regarding the toxicity that relationships can cause. To think there will be no problems in your relationship just because you're with the person you love is unrealistic. I'm sure you already know this. In the previous chapter, I discussed how romance and love aren't consistent. So, no matter how much love you and your partner share, problems will arise, and that's natural. What's not natural, however, is when these problems turn toxic. The moment toxicity, of whatever kind, enters a relationship, it can get really difficult to save it. So, both partners must

55

remain alert and take notice of any issue that might have occurred so that immediate remedial action can be taken. This is why identifying toxic traits in a relationship is so important.

What Makes a Relationship Toxic?

This is a complex question, and there are no textbook answers because toxicity is subjective to a certain extent. However, there are signs of toxicity that are the same for all of us. Some of these include:

- **<u>When your partner is constantly attempting to trap you</u>** – Not everyone will be aware of this tricky behavior, especially at the beginning of a relationship. It might take you a while before you realize how your partner's words are expressed in a specific way that's intended to put you on the spot. It might seem to be harmless when they say, "Well, it seems you had a very cozy evening with your colleague tonight," after the two of you return home from an office party. What you answer will decide the mood for that evening and establish where you both stand as a couple (Young, n.d.).

- **<u>When either of the partners starts denying their needs because the other person doesn't care</u>** – It's indeed unfortunate when a relationship takes a wrong turn and starts deteriorating. When you're with the wrong person, it won't matter what your needs are because, for them, the relationship is only a means to get what *they* want. So, after a point, you'll just stop expressing or even thinking about your needs or opinions because you know your partner doesn't care about them—or you.

- **<u>You feel bad all the time</u>** – You'll know for a fact that the relationship isn't going anywhere good when you start feeling bad all the time. You might be able to see the reasons why this is happening, or it could be something that you can't quite put your finger on, but you're aware that your partner's presence is making you feel bad about yourself and depressed. It's a clear sign of toxicity when your partner's presence stops bringing you any joy.

- **<u>When saying no isn't allowed</u>** – Consent is one of the primary factors of a healthy relationship. No matter how small or how big an issue might be, when one partner isn't okay with it, the other person should never force them to do it. Know for a fact that a relationship is becoming toxic when you notice that giving your consent has stopped meaning anything to your partner.

<u>How to Identify Toxic Relationships</u>

Understanding these concepts won't be enough to avoid toxicity unless you apply them in your everyday life. We're now going to discuss how you can identify toxic relationships.

The primary requirement in identifying whether your relationship is getting toxic is to be aware of exactly what's going on. At times, toxicity may be difficult to discern, but you'll be able to get a sense of it if you don't take anything for granted. At other times, the toxicity could be right in front of your eyes, but it doesn't register because you choose to remain blind to it. I'm not implying that allowing toxicity is your fault. But you're as much a part of this relationship as is your partner. It falls on your shoulders to be aware of everything. You shouldn't be passive initially and then complain afterward about what went wrong. As with anything else in life, you need to be accountable and take responsibility for your role in the situation. The attitude of both partners is important to keep a relationship going.

The next thing that's needed for you to identify whether your relationship is getting toxic is to acknowledge that toxicity is a possibility. Often, people make the mistake of remaining in denial about toxicity because they're afraid to be alone or they're overly dependent on their partner or because they don't want to accept that their relationship isn't healthy and they need to break up. It's common in human psychology for people to try to mend things. But ask yourself, "For how long should I try to do this?" Also, it shouldn't be only you making all the effort.

Most importantly, you deserve better than being depressed all the time. This doesn't mean that you or your partner are bad at relationships, or the relationship has no value or meaning. It could simply be that this is as far as you both were supposed to go together.

Types of Toxic People

There are many types of toxic people. The following are some of the most potent and common ones for you to be aware of:

- **The Belittler** – The belittler is someone who chooses to look down on you for everything you do. In the presence of a belittler, you'll feel you're the one who's always at fault. You'll start feeling you aren't with a romantic partner but with your boss or superior. This will soon start making you feel claustrophobic. A relationship can only work when both partners are given equal respect and opportunities to develop. Disrespecting your partner is cruel and insensitive, and insensitivity is the epitome of toxicity.

- **The Guilt-Inducer** –_Such a partner, will play the game of victimizing themselves all the time so they can put all the blame on you and make you feel guilty. No matter whose fault something is, they'll make sure you feel you should take the blame. Imagine the amount of mental stress you'll be subjected to remaining in a relationship with such an individual.

- **The Codependent Partner** –_Probably one of the most toxic of all relationships is one based on codependency. One partner in a codependent relationship takes zero responsibility for anything and feeds on the other partner's peace of mind. The caretaking half of the couple can experience both emotional and physical strain in trying to provide what their partner wants. It's almost like taking care of a baby but without any growth to provide happiness in return.

- **The Possessive Partner** –_The possessive partner suffers from a lack of self-confidence. As a result, they become paranoid and want to control their mate. They may proclaim this possessiveness is proof of their concern for their partner, but their goal is control. If the possessive partner is disloyal, they'll think their partner is likely to be unfaithful as well. This will make them question all their partner's decisions and want to keep track of everything they're doing—almost like a crazed stalker (Cory, n.d.).

The Symptoms of a Toxic Relationship

Toxicity in a relationship has several important symptoms and signs. Being aware of these can be helpful for you to better identify the presence of toxicity. Some of the most common symptoms of a toxic relationship are:

- **Anger** – Anger on the part of both partners is a symptom of a toxic relationship. You feel anger as a victim of toxicity, and they feel anger as the medium that initiates that toxicity. As a result, there will be ongoing tension between the two of you, and both of you will lose your temper often.

- **<u>Addiction</u>** – A toxic person is more often than not vulnerable to substance abuse. Be aware if this is the reason they're behaving differently or letting their negativities get the better of them when they're with you. Once addiction comes into the equation, many of the good aspects of the relationship can turn bad.

- **<u>Obsession</u>** – A toxic person often becomes obsessed with people and situations so they can be more in control of them. That obsession could be you; it could be how household matters are handled; it could be where the relationship is going. It's natural for a toxic person to try and keep everything under their command, and this can play out as obsession.

- **<u>Feeling manipulated</u>** – Do you feel you're being manipulated by your partner? If that's the case, it could be that your relationship is toxic. Staying together should be about two consenting individuals wanting to do so. Neither of the partners should be manipulating the other as that's insulting and demoralizing.

- **<u>Feeling like a victim</u>** – The moment you start feeling like a victim in your relationship, there's no doubt your partner and the relationship have turned toxic. It may or may not be their intention, but your feeling like a victim proves there's no space for you in that relationship anymore.

- **<u>Overpowering negative emotions</u>** – When a relationship becomes toxic, negative emotions predominate. The one who regards themselves as a victim will feel insulted and undergo psychological torture. The behavior of the toxic partner is proof enough of their negativity. As a result, there's no option but for this particular relationship to primarily function on negative emotions.

- **<u>Gaslighting</u>** – Gaslighting is when a toxic person manipulates you in a way that continuously makes you question your sanity. Such people have many tricks and tactics to assure their manipulations aren't obvious so no one can accuse them. Gaslighting, thus, is never evident on its face. And yet, it's an extremely dangerous and damaging practice that can make the victim question themselves at every turn and destroy their sense of self. Toxic partners often gaslight the other person to get what they want.

The Toxic Relationship Cycle

Understanding the toxic relationship cycle is the only way to remove yourself from it. Let me take you through it in detail by describing the four phases.

- **Phase 1: The Build-Up** - After observing the toxic behavior a few times, you start realizing it's a pattern. Because of this, tension builds up. Maybe it's a sense of walking on eggshells or a sinking plunge in the pit of your stomach that tells you the storm is coming again. Sometimes, this tension can feel unbearable. You know something is going to go wrong, you just don't know when. You try to act as normal as possible, so you don't trigger them.

- **Phase 2: The Incident** - This is when the toxic incident occurs. This could be an explosive situation that keeps recurring or anything that causes constant interruptions in the relationship. When the toxic behavior happens, it's harmful, but you've been here before. The person has yet again, unsurprisingly, failed to change their behavior. These incidents may include arguments, verbal or physical abuse, anger, blaming, threats, or intimidation.

- **Phase 3: Reconciliation** - In this stage, the person responsible for the toxic behavior tries to justify their actions and apologizes. They provide excuses, downplay the incident, and promise it won't happen again. If the apology isn't immediately accepted, they might try to coax forgiveness with gifts and love bombing.

- **Phase 4: Calm** - The last stage of the cycle is calm. In this stage, the storm has settled. Amends were made, and you're back to being the couple you once were before the incident. The relationship appears to be a little more stable, and the incident is forgotten. The toxic partner may make some minor improvements during this period. However, over time, you begin to notice these start to diminish. This is a sign the cycle may be repeating and returning to phase one.

Why Do We Stick with Toxic People?

I'm sure most of us have asked this question either about ourselves or people we know. Leaving a toxic relationship is easier said than done. There are many fundamental reasons why someone would stay in a damaging or unhealthy relationship. Let's explore why this happens.

- **Low self-esteem** – Having low self-esteem is one of the primary reasons people stay in a relationship even when it's toxic. They may fully understand their partner is bad for them, yet they still can't move on because they think they'll never find anyone else or, worse, that they deserve this harmful relationship.

- **Fear of loneliness** – Some people have such an intense fear of loneliness that they compromise their mental and physical health to stay in a negative and toxic relationship. For them, being alone is a terrifying thought, and they'd rather be ill-treated than be alone.

- **Investment** – Some people get so intensely involved with their partner and their relationship that the prospect of losing that emotional and physical investment is overwhelmingly frightening. This is why they decide to stay in a toxic relationship.

- **Need to help or "fix" their partner** – Many people choose to stay in unhealthy relationships out of an inherent need to help or fix their partner. They feel their partner can't save themselves, and they need to come to their rescue. They treat their partner as their responsibility, and it's their job to fix them. Even when they understand that this desire is toxic (and, usually, fruitless), they choose to stay and keep trying.

- **Family and children** – Some people maintain a toxic relationship for the sake of the children due to the belief that the children would be affected negatively by the separation of their parents.

- **Manipulation and entrapment** - Manipulation is a hallmark of emotional abuse within toxic relationships. Many individuals in unhealthy relationships are continuously manipulated to believe that leaving the relationship isn't an option. Quite often, they may feel isolated and distanced from their support network. They may be afraid to leave the relationship because their partner has threatened them.

Living in a toxic relationship is hell, and the sooner you exit and heal from it, the better it will be for you. I understand that it can be extremely difficult to take such a drastic step despite understanding how devastating living in such a situation is. After all, we're talking about leaving the person you love. But the person you should love the most is yourself, and no one is worth putting your mental health at risk. So, take

69

one small step at a time, but make sure you leave such a relationship as soon as possible.

CHAPTER 4: NARCISSISTIC ABUSE

Narcissism is indeed a factor in toxicity, but it has distinctive features that set it apart. You can include narcissism under the big umbrella of toxic behavior in general, but you still need to know what exactly it means to be abused by a narcissist. I've explained in the previous chapters what narcissism is, and I'll describe some of its other aspects in this chapter.

Any kind of toxic abuse is dangerous as it can seriously harm your physical and mental health. It has the potential to impair you psychologically for life. Narcissistic abuse is no exception. It is, at times, even more dangerous than other types of toxicity. A person who's been subject to abuse for a long time might lose their sense of self completely as a result.

In this chapter, I'll talk about the difference between toxicity in general and narcissism in particular so you can identify immediately if you're a. I'll talk you through these concepts in detail to make things clearer.

Signs You're in a Relationship with a Narcissist

It might not be evident at the beginning, but it will eventually have an impact if you're in a relationship with a narcissist. The following are a few of the signs that will clue you in to the fact that you have a narcissistic partner:

Your partner can't deal with feedback – It's a common characteristic of narcissists that they can't deal with feedback or criticism of any kind. Even if it's constructive criticism, they won't want to hear it. You've read the previous chapters, so I'm sure you already know that narcissists suffer from an acute sense of lack deep within themselves. They're never sure of what they want and what they're capable of. Coming from that place, it's only natural that they'll be touchy about anything they perceive as criticism.

Your needs aren't important to them – Another person's needs are never important to a narcissist. They're like horses with blinders on. Their only objective is to make sure their needs are getting satisfied. They have no empathy, so naturally, whether you're getting what you need is of no concern to them. In a relationship with a narcissist, this plays out as you being the one who's always making compromises, and everything happens at your expense.

They're obsessed with the idea of success – A relationship functions on many different levels. The individual growth of both partners is necessary for the couple to grow as a unit. That being said, it shouldn't be a situation where one partner gets so obsessed with the idea of success that the other partner is neglected in the process. A narcissist doesn't even know what true success means because they're too fixated on their own concept of it. In an effort to satisfy their ego, they'll blindly run after their idea of success without looking at anything else. In that case, a relationship can never fully develop or help the individual partners to grow.

They manipulate you – Do you feel you're being manipulated in the relationship you're in? One of the major reasons for this could be that your partner is a narcissist. They have this idea of uplifting their self-image by bringing others down. Their superiority complex plays out as manipulating others, especially people close to them. They put others in constant misery through their tricks and tactics just so they can feel a warped sense of power (Miller, 2021).

Apart from the signs mentioned above, there are other indicators that you're in a narcissistic relationship. Does your partner seem to have a sense of entitlement? Do they believe you're jealous of them? These are signs of narcissism as well.

Now that I've established what you should look for to recognize if you're in a relationship with a narcissist, let me take you through the signs you should look for to determine if you're in an abusive relationship.

Toxicity vs. Abuse

What's the difference between a toxic relationship and an abusive relationship? Many people use these phrases interchangeably to talk about unhealthy or damaging relationships but don't have a clear breakdown as to what constitutes toxic behavior and what constitutes abusive behavior.

Often, there are overlaps with toxic and abusive behaviors – no clear line divides the two. It's all about context: What's happening? Where is it happening? Who's involved? How is it happening, and why? Toxicity and abuse can occur in any relationship – Between lovers, parents and children, colleagues at work, friends and siblings. It can also be very subjective and related to the individual's perception. In one situation, the behavior can be toxic; in another, it can be abusive; and in another, it can be neither.

Like most complexities of life, toxic and abusive behavior exist on a spectrum. To understand where an offense might fall, consider what boundaries were crossed, how many times the behavior was repeated, and the intent of the action. All of these factors can help determine how serious it is.

Some toxic behavior is relatively benign and can be described as disrespectful, a bad habit, or poor choice. If someone does these things once or rarely, it can hardly be considered toxic behavior. Repeatedly doing these things, especially if the individual has been confronted about them in the past, points towards toxic behavior. However, doing these things with an intent to harm (physically, mentally, or emotionally) means the behavior is abusive. Many survivors of psychological abuse can attest that it's the accumulation of "little things" done with the intent to harm that causes anguish.

People nowadays often tag anything as toxic or abusive when something doesn't work out. But you need to know the difference between the two, so you can take the necessary steps to ensure your safety. As important as it is not to tolerate such behaviors, it's also important not to jump to conclusions and be very clear about what's happening. You're in a toxic relationship when you feel there's no space for either of you to grow and when all the fights—even the small ones—cause grave emotional turmoil. Your partner behaves in a toxic manner when they constantly need attention and validation but don't care whether you get the same in return. You're in a toxic relationship when you feel like a victim all the time and are subject to aggressive, passive-aggressive, shaming, or other demeaning behavior when your partner's expectations aren't met.

When you're in an abusive relationship, you feel as if you're being dominated, manipulated, made ill use of, and lied to all the time. Your relationship is abusive when you start feeling that your partner is being hurtful on purpose and is taking calculated steps to make you feel bad in whatever way. It might start with them being only emotionally abusive, but, at some point, the abuse is likely to become physical. Your relationship is abusive when your partner gaslights you and needs to be in control of everything—be it financial, social, or sexual control. They demand to call the shots where the relationship is concerned. An abusive partner will try to belittle you whenever they have the opportunity, making sure you feel pressured and dominated.

Am I in an Abusive Relationship?

As I've mentioned, there's a fine but definitive line between abuse and toxicity. It's vital that you understand the differences because the precautions and techniques you need to tackle each are slightly different.

The following are some of the signs that signal you're in an abusive relationship:

Your relationship has gone through several breakups and makeups – Abusive relationships are never smooth. If you're in such a relationship, chances are you've been through multiple breakups and makeups already. An abusive partner will never be fully satisfied with what you give them, both psychically and emotionally. They'll be forever disappointed and needy. They use the emotional trauma of breakups as a means to further abuse you.

78

They enjoy seeing you go through that pain of breaking up because that's how perverted and twisted their minds are. You'll be at a loss to understand what you're doing wrong. While they'll be deriving pleasure out of torturing you.

Your partner uses "love bombing" to manipulate you – Love bombing is a means of taking advantage of a person's feelings to manipulate and abuse them in ways they don't anticipate to satisfy the ego of the person doing the bombing. Love bombing is a form of codependent relationship, where an abusive partner attempts to make amends for everything they do wrong in the relationship by trying to convince their partner that they love them. This mode of emotional abuse is an effort to convince the partner being abused that they're responsible for everything wrong that happens. It also forces them to be the more responsible and mature partner all the time.

They insist on going with you everywhere –Only someone who doesn't trust you and wants to use your mistakes and vulnerabilities to their advantage to wield power over you will want to be with you at all times (Pugle, 2021). They go with you everywhere not because they love you and can't spend a moment out of your presence you but to make you feel they don't trust you—at all. That's a sign of possible abuse.

Even if you're the abused partner, you still want to please the abuser – One of the ways to become aware of whether you're in an abusive relationship is by asking yourself if you want to please your partner even when you clearly know you're being ill-treated. An abusive partner will make a point of establishing the fact that anything that goes wrong with the relationship is your fault. Whether it's out of blind love or fear of more abuse, you'll unconsciously develop the habit of trying to please your partner in any situation.

Abusive relationships are usually exploitative and very often turn physically violent. However, with the above warnings, I've tried to reveal to you some of the more subtle yet equally damaging signs that you should look for.

Manipulation Tactics

Narcissists have a lot of tricks for manipulating you while forcing you to wear your heart on your sleeve around them. It's their greatest achievement to get you to do what they want you to do, so let's look at some of the ways they go about doing that.

- **Projection** – There are many ways narcissists use projection to manipulate people around them. Their inherent lack of courage and self-confidence makes them deny or avoid any fault of their own and, in turn, try to blame others for everything that goes wrong to satisfy their ego. This type of manipulation might take the form of mimicking someone, exaggerating certain things and ignoring others, or planning a preemptive strike on another to make them uncomfortable or embarrassed. There are many strategies that a narcissist could employ to manipulate their targets through projection.

- **Deliberately making you feel foolish** – One of the most common tactics narcissists use to manipulate you is to deliberately make you feel foolish or guilty. At every moment, they'll question your intelligence and disregard your existence. Remember, whatever the situation, the narcissistic always views you as just a tool to get what they want. By crushing your inner spirit, they hope to make you an emotional vegetable who doesn't have an opinion on anything. As a result, they can have their way with you easily. With a narcissist around, you'll always question yourself and feel stupid about things you haven't even done.

- **Avoiding accountability** – Avoiding accountability is a classic narcissistic characteristic. No matter what they've done that was unsuccessful, embarrassing, or made them look bad, they'll never admit to it. They refuse to take responsibility for anything that doesn't make them look good or feed their ego, and they have clever ways to shift the blame on others. If you're their target, you won't have any idea when or for what you'll receive the blame. The narcissist will have already made you feel so inept that when they shift the blame on you, you feel you're in no position to deny it. You'll be manipulated into believing that you've indeed done that thing, when in reality, you haven't.

- **Destructive conditioning** – Destructive conditioning is yet another tactic that narcissists use to manipulate you. They'll condition your mind, day after day, into believing you're what they're projecting onto you. They'll destroy your sense of self and make sure you can't think rationally by introducing doubt into your mind. When you start a relationship with a narcissist, before you know it, you'll be conditioned to become someone who can be easily molded and who will agree to whatever's being asked of you. Your partner will have complete control over you. After that, your partner won't even need to be present to manipulate you because you'll know what they expect and do it automatically.

Now that you know how a narcissist can manipulate you, let me tell you why many people choose to stay in such a relationship even after becoming aware that it's happening.

Why We Get Stuck in Relationships with Narcissists

It might come as a surprise to you that people stay in a relationship with someone they know is a narcissist, or you might know someone who's remained in such a toxic relationship even after knowing the truth. Yes, people often find it difficult to end this kind of unhealthy relationship, and there are valid reasons for that. I'll explain some of these to you now because it's important that you know what they are to help yourself or someone else escape from such a relationship.

- **Trauma bonding** – Most toxic relationships begin with care and kindness. That's how a toxic person traps you. A narcissistic relationship is no different. So, when the kindness stops and the ill-treatment starts, it takes you by surprise. By now, you've grown attached to that person—whom you still perceive as kind and caring—so you try to rationalize their changed behavior as a way to believe you should still be together. You go into denial and let those initial happy memories of mutual bonding disguise the present trauma.

- **Loss of self** – A victim of a narcissistic relationship might find it difficult to leave it because, in all probability, they've lost all sense of courage and self-assurance by now. As I've already mentioned, a narcissist manipulates their victim by crushing their spirit. So, by the time the victim understands what's going on, they can't imagine living without that person. They've been subjected to abuse for so long that they've become habituated to it

- **The dream** – A relationship is a drama involving primarily two people. It might sound stupid or absurd, but for the victim in a relationship with a narcissist, one of the main reasons for sticking with such a person is the constant dream of returning to the good old days. These relationships almost always start on an excellent note. Those happy memories are so strong and vivid that the victim will try their best to believe that, eventually, they and their partner will once again be how they were in those blissful days. They'll continue dreaming that the happy days will return, and that's what makes them stay and suffer.

- **<u>Lack of support</u>** – When a person has been in a toxic relationship with a narcissist for a long time, it's often the case that the narcissist has cut off the other person's sources of external support, so they believe they're trapped. The victim, in all probability, will have no source of financial or emotional support from anyone else. So, even if they think of breaking up, they won't be able to do so as there's no place for them to go.

- **<u>Investing too much in the relationship</u>** – More often than not, the person who's the victim in a toxic relationship will have invested themselves too much in their partner and the relationship—and a narcissist will make sure their partner invests too much. Maybe they pretend to do the same—for a while—so their intentions are never questioned. But if the victim thinks of breaking up, their emotional investment will backfire on them. Emotional investment tells them not to give up and wait a while longer. This increases the suffering even more.

- **Worrying about what others might think** — We're often trapped by the burden of, "What will people think?" This can prevent a person from taking a step like breaking up. A victim might think they'll be laughed at, talked about, or blamed. On top of this, their self-confidence has already been destroyed by their narcissistic partner, so they become anxious about what people will think.

- **Thinking the abuse is deserved** — When someone has been the victim of narcissistic abuse for a long time, they're manipulated into thinking they deserve their ill-treatment. They start thinking that it's meant to be. They try to hold on because they have genuine feelings for their partner. And so, no matter what treatment they get in return, they believe it's bad luck, or they deserve it.

If narcissistic abuse continues, it can affect you for your entire life, as I've mentioned. Often, the victim doesn't even realize what they're going through because they're so manipulated. However, let's suppose you've come to recognize you're involved with a narcissist, or you know someone who's realized this. In that case, it's your responsibility to take the necessary actions to bring this to a stop immediately.

CHAPTER 5: ENDING THE TOXIC CYCLE

In the previous chapters, I talked about the various aspects of a toxic relationship. If you recognized yourself as you read, now's the time to take those crucial measures to end this toxic cycle. You might know what's going on, and you might also understand your own psyche or that of the other person concerned. But unless you start taking conscious and voluntary steps to put an end to this, nothing will improve. Nothing good can come from just knowing what the situation is. Change depends on you taking a stand and making sure you end this.

Be it narcissistic abuse or any other form of toxicity, it won't stop on its own. On the contrary, it will most likely intensify as time goes by. The abuser will accumulate more power over the victim, and the victim will gradually lose themselves and their sense of agency in that process. A toxic relationship can be viewed as a situation in which the balance of the scales of power gradually shifts to the side of the abuser until that person dominates the other. Unless the victim takes a firm stand for themselves, this imbalance of power will continue. In earlier chapters, I talked about the causes of and reasons for toxicity, narcissism, and abuse. In this chapter, I'll be talking about various ways by which you can end the toxic cycle and free yourself from an abusive relationship.

Self-Reflection

The first thing I'll be talking about is self-reflection. Without reflecting on yourself, you won't make any individual progress, and you certainly won't be able to find the strength to leave a toxic relationship. So let me take you through why self-reflection is necessary and its process.

When it comes to self-reflection, the first thing you need to focus on is shame and fear. You need to understand that these emotions play a crucial role in the lives of all human beings. It's only natural for a person who's been a victim of toxicity for a long time to feel afraid and ashamed. This can happen for various reasons. The toxic and abusive partner might have given more than enough reasons to feel ashamed. The abusive person might have insulted you in public or embarrassed you at every opportunity. At the same time, they might have abused the victim emotionally and physically, creating fear.

When you realize it's time for you to step out of such a toxic relationship, unless you get to know yourself in depth and explore all your emotions, you won't be able to make a complete break from the toxic person. Only when you fully acknowledge what you're feeling will you be able to put that toxicity in your past and move on.

First, you need to ask yourself specifically what it is

that you're feeling afraid of or ashamed about. It's critical not to disregard any emotion and understand that every feeling is valid. The final step is to come to terms with your emotions so you can feel confident to take control of your life.

When you've discovered and acknowledged your fears and those things that you're ashamed of, the next thing you must realize is that they won't disappear just because you want them to unless you take action. In all probability, they're hampering you in your daily life and causing difficulties in your day-to-day activities. This is where self-reflection comes in. You might hide something from the entire world, but know this for a fact: You can't hide it from yourself and expect anything to change. Sit with yourself and think through what you're feeling. Make sure you're completely honest with yourself and don't hide anything. Try to understand what triggers you. Self-reflection is the primary procedure for cleansing your soul from all the ill-treatment and torture you've been through. That's what I mean when I say that you have to be empathetic toward yourself. When you don't disregard what you've been through and give yourself full credit for being courageous enough to consider moving out of it, this will make it possible for you to successfully put your past behind you (Sutton, 2021).

When you've taken this first and essential step of self-reflection, you'll likely encounter a flood of emotions. These are often emotions that your toxic partner has been causing you to suppress for so long. These need to come out, but, most importantly, they need to be expressed in a healthy way. That's where skillful communication comes into the conversation.

Healthy Communication Skills

Communication is of prime importance when ending the toxic cycle and bidding goodbye to that unhealthy life for good. You need to be able to communicate with your loved ones so you can move on from everything traumatic that's happened in the past. Below I've listed some strategies for positively communicating with others without allowing your pent-up anger, frustration, and irritation to get in the way.

- **Be emotionally aware** – The first step to take when communicating with others is to be emotionally aware. Whether you're communicating with your abusive partner, your therapist, or your family or friends, you need to be mindful of the situation. Be present in that moment. Your emotions might get the better of you, and your fears might threaten to take your courage away. But know this truth: The very fact that you've gathered the courage to step out of this abusive relationship is proof that you're fully capable of taking control of your life. So, don't let thoughts of the past overpower you, and instead, be aware of what's going on in front of you. That way, you'll better control your emotions and remain in the present. As a result, you'll communicate better.

- **Organize your thoughts** – Given that you've been a victim of a narcissistic and toxic relationship for a long time, it's only natural that you'll have many things to say when given the chance. Your emotions and feelings have been disregarded, and your thoughts weren't

94

paid any attention. Now that you have the chance to express yourself, all these thoughts are trying their best to come out all at once. However, you need to give each thought its due importance, so take time to address each one carefully and completely so you can communicate it as clearly as possible. This way, you can express fully everything you want and need to say, and your mind, situation, and exact feelings will be fully understood by the person listening to you.

- **Use simple and clear language** – When you're talking about something unpleasant, it's only natural that you'll feel tense and might start mixing up your words, given that your emotions are all over the place. You might find it difficult to get across to others what you're feeling. It's important to calm down, focus, and speak in a clear and concise manner. No matter who you're talking to—your therapist, the police, or someone else—they need to understand exactly what's happened and how you feel so the necessary actions can be taken. You need your voice to be heard, so it's essential to use simple and straightforward language. Take a deep breath, sort out the thoughts in your mind, and then start talking. That way, you'll be able to communicate better, and everything that you have to say will be clear to the person listening to you.

- **Validate your feelings** – If you've spent a lot of time with a toxic person, it's a given that they never treated you with the respect you deserve. Your needs were never even considered, much less met, and your feelings were disregarded. As a result, you became accustomed to believing that your feelings don't matter. You became habituated to not investing your feelings with the importance they deserve. Now you realize this is unhealthy and that you must acknowledge and accept your often conflicting emotions. Unless you validate your feelings, you'll be doing yourself an injustice. You must give credence to everything you feel, which will allow others to begin to comprehend what you've been through and its effect on you. I understand that this is easier said than done, given your past traumatic history. But it's never too late to start doing the right thing. Start treating yourself the way you want others to treat you, and see what a big difference that makes. Whenever you communicate with someone, never denigrate your feelings. This is good practice for regaining your power.

- **Try to keep the stress in check** – Stress can cause a great deal of damage, which I'm sure you're already aware of. When communicating with someone regarding your toxic relationship, it's natural to be stressed because all those traumatic memories are present in your mind. It's reasonable that you don't want to remember these, and they can also serve as triggers that create additional stress in people who are trying their best to put their past behind them. Stress can make communicating difficult, but you're aware of this. You might fail to say what you needed to, and you might feel much gets lost. This is why you need first to get a firm grip on your stress and envision what you want to say clearly. When you're sure that you have the stress under control, proceed with what you have to say. That way, you'll be aware of the points you want to make and how you want to make them to communicate your feelings properly (Robinson, Segal, & Smith, 2020).

- **Own what's yours** – Owning what's yours, especially when you've decided to leave a toxic relationship, is crucial. If you've been a victim of toxic abuse, I'm sure you know better than others just how much you've been denied what's yours for all that time. Be it your feelings or something else, none of it got the attention it deserved. Now's the time to claim what's yours. When you communicate with someone, make sure you're crystal clear from the get-go about those things that you won't compromise and everything that's happened to you. Every one of your emotions is valid—both good and bad. For all this while, you've accepted the bad, so now it's time for you to do the same with the good. You need to own everything to be able to accept the past and move on to a future that doesn't include compromising who you are.

All the points mentioned above are healthy ways to communicate your feelings to others successfully. If you don't choose healthy ways of communication, it won't be easy to express your thoughts and emotions to others clearly. You won't be doing justice to yourself unless you adopt healthy ways of interaction. Now that you've decided to put the negative and toxic past behind you, it's your responsibility to communicate in ways that add positivity to your life.

Next, I'll talk about what's most imperative for moving out of a toxic relationship—the methods by which you can free yourself from a toxic person—which, after all, is the ultimate objective.

How to Become Free of a Toxic Person

One of the main objectives of my book is to provide you with solutions for freeing yourself from the toxic person that's has been adding misery to your life. And so, here I am, keeping that promise. We'll now explore some of the most effective ways to successfully leave a toxic person and end the toxic cycle.

Confront Your Reality

The first thing you must do is acknowledge and confront the reality of your situation. Accept that you're in a toxic relationship. The more in denial you are, the longer it will take to remove this person from your life. Of course, no one wants such a thing to happen to them, but now that it has, instead of letting fear or shame overwhelm you, accept the situation, and don't waste a single moment in working to gain your freedom. Confronting your reality not only means being realistic about the toxic relationship but also regaining respect for your life and achieving mental peace. It means you're not giving up and have decided to stop giving that person another chance. Now, you know the reality—which is, they're not going to change. With this acceptance of the situation, it will become easier to handle whatever's going on and take the necessary steps.

Be Accountable

When you're reviewing all the ways in which you've been wronged, you must figure out your own responsibility as well. I'm in no way saying you're toxic like your partner. However, every human being has their share of vulnerabilities, and so do you. That's why you need to not only eliminate that toxic person from your life but address your part in agreeing to tolerate the situation as long as you did. You must accept that you're not perfect and acknowledge the mistakes you've made. When you do that, letting go of that person who's so unhealthy for you is easier. You'll better understand the dynamics of the relationship, and you'll also learn that you can no longer compromise who you are. What's more, you'll be more cautious about whom you trust and how you behave in the future, so the same mistakes aren't repeated.

Make Yourself a Priority

You must understand your worth before you even try to free yourself from a toxic individual. A toxic person will have you believe you're no good and easily replaceable. It's high time you realize this is absolutely not the case. You must make yourself your highest priority so that, henceforth, no one ever dares to ill-treat you. Others often treat us in the way we treat yourselves. You have to make sure you take care of all your emotional and physical needs so no one can ever make you feel any less. Only when your mind and body feel at complete ease with yourself will you be able to successfully leave a negative relationship. You'll fully understand your worth, and you won't let anyone take you for granted (Firestone, 2017).

Find Support

Try to find as much external support as possible when you separate yourself from a toxic person. Toxic people usually hold a lot of power over us, so make sure you're financially stable and have a secure place to go before you walk out on them. Make sure you have both legal and medical help so that, once you're out of there, that toxic person can cause you no harm. An abusive person may go to great lengths to cause harm to their victim. They have a huge ego, which might make them want to seek revenge for you leaving them. That's why you need to have proper support to ensure your safety.

Set Boundaries

Setting boundaries is one of the most important things we do in life. Any person coming into your life should know what your boundaries are and what will happen

102

if they cross them. This helps people know what's acceptable and, more importantly, it helps you avoid unnecessary problems. Whenever the toxic person in your life crosses the line, make them aware of this and the consequences if they continue to disrespect your boundaries. The more professionally you behave toward them, the easier it will be for you to control the situation.

Encourage Them to Get Help

It's often difficult to understand why people behave in toxic ways. But it might help to consider that they might be dealing with some personal challenges that cause them to lash out. This doesn't excuse problematic behavior, but it can help explain it. Encourage them to talk to a therapist about why they act the way they do.

Leave if Necessary

In most cases, it's necessary to leave a toxic relationship in order to heal and move forward with your life. A relationship only works for as long as both parties want it, but it also shouldn't continue if either partner is being abused. The moment one of the partners decides to no longer participate in improving the relationship, it often ends unless a substantial effort is made to address the problems. This is usually more successful if couples counseling is involved. If your partner has made you believe you can't leave them—or threatens you if you consider leaving them—you need to realize this person is manipulating you. If you've genuinely tried to change the dynamics of the relationship and diminish the toxicity and nothing has worked, it's time to leave. You deserve so much more than an overbearing person trying to take advantage of you. You don't need to explain anything to anyone when your safety and mental peace are at stake.

You should always be your top priority. Never let anyone make you believe otherwise. Any relationship—whether with a family member, peer, boss, or romantic partner—should never jeopardize your relationship with yourself. When a toxic person threatens to disrupt that balance, the best thing for you to do is remove yourself from that toxic cycle. Throughout this chapter, I've discussed ways to regain control of your life.

I hope this chapter has been helpful in providing you with the answers you've been looking for in learning how to end the toxic cycle.

CHAPTER 6: HEALING AND RECOVERY AFTER THE STORM

Being in an abusive or otherwise toxic relationship, for whatever amount of time, can be compared to living within a hurricane. Every day, you faced the storm, and I'm sure that's left you drained. However, the very fact that you're acknowledging what's happened and are now seeking answers to how to put this experience in your past shows how courageous you are. I'm so proud of you. It's not easy to exit a toxic relationship, as I've discussed at length in the previous chapters. But coming out of an abusive or toxic relationship is just the beginning. What comes next is healing from it.

As difficult as it is to live with that negativity, it's also difficult to heal from it. The reasons are obvious. Being subjected to toxicity and a prolonged exposure to negative energy can make any person incapable of accepting positivity for a long time after that. It takes intense work to undo the events of the past for a person to regain their self-confidence and take steps on their own behalf. This is exactly where the challenge lies. You have to give yourself a chance to live the life you deserve by allowing yourself to heal. I'm sure this chapter will provide you with the needed answers you've been seeking about how to heal and recover after the storm.

Recovering Your Lost Self

As I've stated previously, the first step in taking back your life is acknowledging you're in a toxic relationship. The second step is to make up your mind about whether you want to stay in that relationship. When you've decided that now is the time to stop allowing that toxic person to take advantage of you, the next step is to leave that relationship and heal yourself so you can move on. As you learned earlier in this book, the toxic person makes you lose touch with yourself as a means of making it easier for them to manipulate you. You need to recover from the effects of this abuse so you can heal completely (Ripes, 2021).

Let's discuss how you can do that. Here are a few things to keep in mind:

- **Don't expect closure** – Don't commit the mistake of expecting closure with your toxic ex. They didn't care about you when the relationship was alive. Naturally, they'll be even less concerned about your well-being now that you've broken up. I know that getting closure feels necessary, but not at the cost of getting hit by that toxic storm again, right? So, just let it be, and don't allow yourself to get tangled in that mess again.

- **Feel all your emotions** - To recover your self-esteem and self-confidence, you need to let yourself feel everything—both good and bad. Ignoring the bad isn't the way to go to feel better. Let the pain come so you can process and release it. Let yourself feel whatever arises, for only then will you be completely free from that past manipulation.

- **Don't check in with your ex** – No matter how tempting it is, resist the urge to check in with your ex. Remember, they're skilled at manipulating you. It might seem that checking in with them is harmless, but one thing may lead to another and, before you know it, you'll have taken two steps backward, thinking you're taking one step forward. When you're trying to recover from a toxic relationship, it's essential that you not go near any negative influence. Let yourself only be around situations and people that are positive.

- **Give yourself time** – You must be patient with yourself if you want to heal. Healing is a time-consuming process, and it won't be successful if you push yourself too hard or become impatient. You need to understand that your mind and body need to come to terms with your new life. Only then will you be able to respond positively to it. You need time to trust again and to regain your confidence. Start by taking baby steps and then move into longer strides. The kinder you are to yourself, the easier it will be for you to heal fully. You'll then be able to release the negativity within and move on.

Now that you know what to do to successfully recover, the next step is to learn how to start loving yourself again. You need to take care of yourself so you can believe that love and kindness still exist. Let's discuss what will help you do that.

Relearning What Love Looks Like Through Self-Care

There are certain things you should be aware of as you're trying to heal after a toxic relationship so you know you're taking a step in the right direction and aren't letting the remnants of that toxicity continue to have an impact on your life. One of the primary focuses in healing is to take care of yourself. You never got the love and care you deserve during the time you were in that toxic relationship. Now that you're trying to heal, you have to make sure you restore everything that was taken from you.

Take Control of Your Body and Mind

Your first and foremost goal should be to take back control of what was taken from you – control of both your mind and of your body. A toxic partner does their best to take this away from you. They don't allow you to grow in any way, and they dominate you in every aspect of your life. So, you have to get beyond that atmosphere of manipulation and let yourself realize it's you who's now in charge of steering your life. Your mind and body have been battered. Give them the time they need to heal completely. During that time, make sure you aren't pushing yourself too hard. Take the time to replenish yourself with all the positivity around you—and, now that you're free of the abusive relationship, you'll find there's lots of positivity in the world. When you heal properly, you emerge stronger from that dark cave of negativity. Let only positive people, thoughts, and experiences have the ability to impact your mind.

Practice Healthy Coping Skills

The next thing you need to do is start practicing healthy coping skills. I'll talk more about this in detail later in this chapter. Coping skills vary in their degree of true benefit. Some are outright harmful—for example, alcoholism or nicotine addiction. You might initially think that resorting to alcohol, drugs, or other methods is an effective way to keep your mind off those dark memories. The problem is you're replacing one kind of abuse with another in an attempt to deal with the repercussions of a toxic relationship. In your helplessness, you might develop other toxic habits that can harm or impair you. That's what I mean by learning healthy coping skills that allow you to fill your life with positivity and progress.

Be More Accountable

Learning to love yourself also means being your biggest critic. Your life is a continuous journey that will invariably have a lot of ups and downs. There will be times when you feel proud of yourself, and there will be times when you regret doing a particular thing. This is all a part of the journey, and you can't disregard or deny any of it. So, instead of trying to ignore the not-

113

so-good parts, the best thing you can do is to be your own best critic and be accountable for areas in which you need improvement. By looking at yourself honestly, you'll discover those things that you need to work on more and perhaps change so you can grow. Being accountable also makes you realize that not everyone who's toxic is conscious of it. Some people don't have bad intentions, but their behavior or even just their presence can be toxic for you. So, along with understanding yourself, you start understanding others better as well.

Taking care of yourself—both your mind and your body—is the ultimate act of self-love. The fact that you've decided that from now on you won't allow anyone to take you for granted shows that you're giving yourself the respect you deserve. Taking a vow that you won't permit anyone to mistreat you shows that you regard your well-being above all others. It shows that you love and care for yourself and will never let anyone take that away from you ever again. You'll be able to heal fully when you embrace yourself. All the scars from your toxic relationship will eventually disappear when you envelope yourself with self-love.

Let me now share some of the techniques and exercises to practice to help you heal.

8 Ways to Cleanse Your Mind and Your Life After Ending a Toxic Relationship

1. Keep positive people around you – One of the best practices to indoctrinate into your mind while you're trying to heal is having positive people around you. This could be friends, family, or anyone you feel comfortable and warm around. These are the people who'll remind you often how special you are and that there's nothing wrong with you. They'll help you overcome those painful memories of your past relationship that may make you feel terrible even now. They'll help restore your hope that not everyone out there is bad. You'll slowly learn to trust yourself and others more. It's through the influence of these positive people that you'll give life and love another chance. The effects of the toxicity you experienced will start to diminish in the presence of the positivity these people will surround you with (Fuller, 2018).

115

2. Practice self-care – This is the time to be selfish. And honestly, there's nothing wrong with that. You just went through a traumatic experience, and the last thing you should do right now is focus on someone else. Self-care might look different to different people because what it means for each of us is entirely subjective. For you, it could be, for example, reading a good book, while for another it could be shopping for a gift for someone they care about. For somebody else, it's listening to music. Traveling might be the best self-care for yet another person. So, as far as self-care is concerned, I'm not going to give you any specific instructions. Instead, I request that you sit with yourself and think about what makes you happy. What is that thing you truly love doing that gives you peace? Whatever answer you get, I want you to take a solemn vow to practice that. Remember, what you know is good for you may not make sense to anyone else. But if it makes you happy—and is good for you—do it. Do yourself this favor and engage whatever makes you happy. Eat healthily and involve yourself in healthy physical activities that help your body to stay fit. Be kind to yourself because you deserve it.

3. Forgive yourself – Stop being angry at yourself. You did nothing wrong. This can be incredibly hard to do. However, the last thing you want is to live the rest of your life beating yourself over something that's not meant to define you. While it's essential to share and express what's happened to you, it's also important to take care of yourself while you're moving forward.

4. Don't allow self-doubt or regret to set in – One of the things that you should never do is allow regret or self-doubt to set in. I know that's easier said than done, given that a toxic person destroys your sense of self-confidence. Staying with them makes you question yourself all the time, and it indeed takes a lot of time once they're out of your life to regain what you've lost. That's the reason you need to consciously remind yourself that your situation wasn't your fault. The moment you let regret take hold of you, it will grip you hard and make healing very difficult. If you allow self-doubt to set in, you'll find it harder to accept yourself or the actions you're taking. It's only human to make mistakes, and you need to accept that. The only way you'll heal from all the trauma is when you accept what happened and not punish yourself for it.

You'll heal when you decide not to let history repeat itself while also not disregarding it.

5. Take time before starting another relationship – It's essential when you're just emerging from a toxic relationship to you give yourself enough time before you get into another relationship. There's a misconception among many people that entering a rebound relationship as a way to forget one's ex is a good idea. A rebound relationship often means seeing someone just to have fun and not get deeply involved with them emotionally. This may seem like a way to quickly distance yourself from the pain of the previous relationship, but this isn't recommended because you're using one person to get over someone else. Going for a rebound relationship is an unkind, messy choice, so don't do it. All it does is complicate matters for yourself and often deeply hurts the other person. Apart from that, it isn't wise to jump into a relationship without knowing you're fully ready for it. Let yourself grow and breathe on your own, and let your heart heal. That will take some time, and you should give yourself that much-needed time.

<u>6. Communicate your feelings</u> – Communicating your feelings is a must when you're trying to heal and move on. As long as the other person is someone you fully trust, there shouldn't be anything to stop you from letting it all out. You were insulted, emotionally tortured, and disregarded for all this time. This must have caused you a great deal of agony. You might not have been able to let those feelings out for all the time you were with that toxic person. Just because that person isn't in your life anymore doesn't mean that those feelings have disappeared. They're still there, and they need to be expressed. The sooner you find someone with whom you can safely share your feelings, the easier it will be to heal. You simply have to communicate and stop suffering alone. You aren't alone, and don't let anyone tell you otherwise. Be it with your therapist or your best friend, communicate exactly how that toxic person made you feel. Release all the negativity from your system, and let positive energy flow into you.

<u>7. Think of yourself not as a victim but as a survivor</u> – This means seeing yourself as a strong person who's capable of getting through anything. It

119

can be hard to get out of a victim mindset — but you can do it. Staying in the victim mindset can prevent you from finding healthy romantic relationships in the future or trusting yourself.

8. Seek professional help – Seeking professional help may be necessary, especially if the pain and other emotions are too much to process by yourself. You never know how a toxic person will impact your life or to what degree that prolonged exposure to toxicity has changed you. So, during the period of moving on, when you notice you're finding it challenging to tackle everything on your own, don't just endure by yourself and expect everything to magically become all right. Seek the help of a therapist if you need to. Find a mental health professional who specializes in relationship abuse. There may be aspects of your trauma that friends and family won't be able to help you with. If that's the case, you need a professional who can guide you in the right direction. Give yourself this opportunity so your past experiences don't have the power to continue to hurt you, and you can find a healthy way to express those negative emotions.

When you regain the confidence to accept and love yourself again, you need to make sure you learn how to sustain your self-confidence so that, in the future, you don't get involved in another destructive relationship like you had with your ex. To do this, you need to develop goals and values within yourself.

Developing Goals for Your New Life

Now that you're out of a toxic relationship, you need to set specific goals and focus on certain values that will help you focus on yourself and your well-being. Changing your perspective can change your entire life for the better, and that's what you should aim for. Some of the ways you can develop goals and values include:

- **Never accept anything less than what you deserve**. Many people will come your way, who aren't destructive or toxic, but they're also not as good as you deserve. Just because they're not causing you any immediate harm, that's not a reason to jump into a relationship with them. Set a healthy relationship standard for yourself and stick to it. Don't make yourself available to everyone.

- **Focus on you**. From now on, your primary goal should be your well-being and not allowing that to be jeopardized for any reason. Make sure you aren't leaving any stones unturned when it comes to yourself. Eat healthy, exercise, do things that enhance you emotionally and spiritually, and only let those people into your inner circle who add value to your life.

- **Learn to let go**. Although this is easier said than done, start taking small steps and practice letting go of things—even if they aren't toxic, but definitely if they are—that aren't adding value to your life. Anyone or anything you let in should have some purpose. If they don't, you should let them go. Life is too short to waste time and feelings on anything that doesn't nurture you.

- **Forgive yourself**. No matter how much you believe you contributed to the difficulties in your past relationship that caused it to turn out the way it did, you simply have to forgive yourself if you want to heal. Your regret and your guilt might be justified, but you shouldn't hold on to them. Instead, learn from them, and eventually, let them go. Unless you forgive yourself, loving yourself and allowing yourself to grow will be difficult.

As I've already mentioned earlier in this chapter, truly healing is necessarily a time-consuming process, but that's the only way you'll truly be whole again. All you need to do is gradually build your self-confidence so you can once again love yourself. When you realize how special you are, all your efforts will go into developing who you truly are and not allowing any toxic person to enter your life. What's happened can't be undone, but what you *can* do is make your future much more rewarding and peaceful. The storm has passed, and it's time for you to breathe and be happy.

CONCLUSION

Thank you for making it through to the end of *How to Deal With Toxic People and Relationships*. I hope it was informative and provided you with all the tools you need to help you identify, escape, and heal from toxic people and toxic relationships.

I hope I was able to provide you with the answers that you were looking for. The intention in writing this book was to delve into the various facets of toxic relationships so that you, the reader, would have the tools to better escape from or avoid toxic experiences in your life.

In chapter one, I talked about what characterizes toxic and narcissistic behavior. I discussed how you can recognize such people and why toxic people are the way they are. My intention for that chapter was to help you recognize the red flags you might have been missing and take you on a quick tour into the psyche of toxic people so you can deal with them better.

After helping you recognize such people, in chapter two, I talked about all the shades of a relationship—the good, the bad, and the ugly. Many of us might be in a toxic relationship without realizing it, given that toxic people are excellent manipulators. I hope chapter two provided you with answers regarding how to differentiate between codependent and interdependent relationships and what kinds of attachments you should look for and avoid.

After discussing what makes a relationship the way it is, I discussed the nature of a toxic relationship in chapter three. I pointed out that the very fact that narcissists and abusive people can manipulate you into believing that what's happening in the relationship is okay and that you deserve the treatment you receive is at the heart of toxicity. I talked about the symptoms, signs, and reasons why a relationship can become toxic. I hope that chapter helped you understand the basics of gaslighting and problems like love addiction, which were also discussed in detail.

This book aims to make you feel that you're not alone and to assure you that the answers you're looking for are indeed available. In chapter four, I discussed at length the difference between toxicity and abuse to help you understand what happens to you in a toxic relationship and how to take the necessary steps to heal from that. It's natural to get stuck in a relationship with a narcissist because narcissists can take away your agency and destroy your self-confidence. Sometimes people get trapped in a toxic relationship because they've invested themselves in it completely. They hold on to the dream that their partner will change into a good person and their relationship will work. Every relationship is unique, which is why I talked about the different reasons why a person might put up with that toxicity. I hope you were able to resonate with one or more of the reasons I mentioned.

The purpose of the first four chapters was to set the premise of the problem, and the last two chapters were meant to provide you with solutions. Chapter five talked about how you can break the toxic cycle once you know what it is and have also acknowledged that you're engaged in a toxic relationship. The first step of breaking the toxic cycle is to self-reflect and identify the things you can change about yourself, so you're no longer vulnerable to toxic people and situations. The next thing is to establish healthy communication skills to help yourself come to terms with what's happened and move on. Apart from these, I discussed several more steps in detail, like setting proper boundaries and making yourself your top priority. I tried to respond to any doubts you may have by covering as many feelings and situations as possible that a person might go through while trapped in such a relationship.

I've dedicated the last chapter to your healing after the storm has passed. This book has been a progressive journey of everything that a person goes through—both physically and emotionally—in a toxic relationship and its aftermath. It takes a lot of courage to work through the trauma of something like that and allow yourself to heal.

Since you made it to the end of the book, I'm sure you're one of those courageous people who have the intention of not allowing yourself to continue to suffer but to free yourself from a toxic situation and heal. The human psyche is complex, and recovering from something so sinister takes time and effort. In the book's final chapter, I talked about various techniques for emerging from the negativity you've been subjected to. I provided various self-care habits and discussed ways by which you can recover your sense of self.

I've dedicated the final section to focus on the importance of having a definitive goal and positive values in your life to help you to emerge from that dark phase. All of us have at one time or another been involved in a toxic relationship, and that's why it's crucial that you realize you're not at fault. You have every right to lead a beautiful life. Whether you want that only for yourself or you want someone beside you is solely up to you. But I want you to know that just because something unfortunate happened once doesn't mean it will happen again. With proper precautions, you'll be able to steer clear of toxic people. I also urge you to never give up on yourself and believe that you deserve happiness. You deserve to be loved for who you are, and you should never settle for anything less.

Thank you again for taking the time to read this book so patiently. Helping you when you need it is my joy and privilege. I wish you all the best.

One more thing

If you enjoyed this book and found it helpful, I'd be very grateful if you'd post a short review on Amazon. Your support does make a difference, and I read all the reviews personally so I can get your feedback and make this book even better. I love hearing from my readers, and I'd really appreciate it if you leave your honest feedback.

Thank you for reading!

BONUS CHAPTER

I would like to share a sneak peek into another one of my books that I think you will enjoy. The book is titled ***"The Keys to Being Brilliantly Confident and More Assertive: A Vital Guide to Enhancing Your Communication Skills, Getting Rid of Anxiety, and Building Assertiveness."***

All of us can think of times when we know we should speak up, but we don't. When we feel like we're being taken advantage of, but we just accept it. Later, we kick ourselves, thinking: "If only I would have said something!"

If this sounds like you, look no further! This book serves as a complete guide to understanding assertiveness and becoming more assertive in your own life.

Using practical exercises and techniques, it will teach you how to stand up for what you believe in, ask for what you want, and say no to what you don't want in a way that's confident, calm, and respectful. This book will also show you how to increase your self-confidence and your self-worth.

This book is for:

- People who would like to massively boost their assertiveness
- People who would like to learn how to deal with conflicts
- People who would like to communicate with confidence and charisma
- New managers who need to be more assertive with their team.
- Emerging leaders who want to communicate more clearly and confidently.

- Introverted people who need to set boundaries and say "no."
- Passive communicators who want to speak more directly and honestly.
- People who have difficulty protecting their time, priorities, and goals.
- People who need to set stronger boundaries.
- People who are tired of being a doormat and taking a passive role in relationships
- People who are afraid of standing up for themselves
- People who are tired of being controlled and dominated
- People who struggle with knowing their worth.

This book will teach you the following:
- How to be an Assertive Communicator
- How to Communicate with Confidence and Charisma
- Highly Effective Techniques to Deal with Any Conflict in Your Personal & Professional Life

- How to Have an Assertive Body Language
- How to Speak Up, Share Your Ideas & Opinions in A Persuasive, Calm & Positive Way
- How to Say "no" and establish boundaries without Looking Selfish
- How to Reduce Discomfort When Talking to People
- How to Overcome your fears and limiting beliefs about being assertive
- How to better manage conflict and difficult conversations

Learning how to be more assertive can massively improve your relationships and your overall sense of self-confidence. When you can express yourself assertively and speak up for yourself, other people will respect you more. Even more importantly, you will respect yourself more. Once you start improving your assertiveness, incredible things will happen in your life.

Enjoy this free chapter!

All of us can think of times when we know we should speak up, but we don't. When we feel like we're being taken advantage of, but we just accept it. Later, we kick ourselves, thinking: "If only I would have *said something*!"

This book will help you if you are a person who feels like you need to increase your assertiveness, to improve your communication skills, to better deal with conflict, to improve your level of confidence and to be a better leader. In this book, you will learn how to improve all of these skills and more!

The purpose of this book is to serve as a complete guide to help you understand what assertiveness is and how you can become more assertive in your own life. Using practical exercises and techniques will teach you how to stand up for what you believe, ask for what you want and need, and say no to what you don't want in a way that's confident, calm, and respectful. This book will also be your guide for increasing self-confidence and self-worth. By reading this book, you will improve your life, gain more control over your life, improve your communication skills and your interpersonal skills and be more successful in both your personal life and your work life.

Before we begin delving into how you can start to take action, we are going to look at an important theory related to changing oneself. This theory comes down to your mindset. The type of mindset that you employ has a massive impact on your life and your growth as a person. There is something called a Growth Mindset, which is an essential piece of this book and your goals of changing yourself. The **'growth mindset'** is a term that was coined by Carol Dweck, who is a renowned professor at multiple universities, including Columbia University, Harvard University, and the University of Illinois. Her research with Angela Lee Duckworth stated that intelligence is not a key indicator of success. They believed that success depends on whether or not a person has a *growth mindset*. A **'fixed mindset'** is the opposite of a growth mindset. A fixed mindset is a term for when a person believes that their intelligence and skills are fixed traits and that they are not able to be changed. People of this mindset believe that they have what they have, and that's it.

138

Knowing this fact and the proof it provides can help you to feel empowered and hopeful. If you struggle with your confidence and your level of assertiveness, understanding that it is a skill that can be learned and honed over time means that this will not remain something that you struggle with anymore. By picking up this book, you are already taking the first steps involved in changing your life by becoming a more confident and more assertive person. If this were an innate characteristic, this would mean that it would be difficult for you to change. Take comfort in this fact and continue reading this book as we will discuss exactly how you can make these changes in your life.

By the end of this book, you will be well on your way to changing your life for the better in numerous ways, and you will be wondering how you ever lived without this information. There is no better time than now to change the parts of yourself that you wish were different.

What Does It Mean to Be Assertive?

To begin, we are going to look at what assertiveness is,

as well as some points related to assertiveness so that you can get a better idea of what exactly this word means. By first making sure that you understand assertiveness, this will help you to understand what benefits can come of assertiveness and how it will benefit you.

What Is Assertiveness?

Assertiveness is being able to use effective communication as well as negotiation, in order to remain true to your personal needs and boundaries when interacting with other people. Being assertive isn't about aggressively putting up walls and shutting people out, contrary to popular belief. There is no shame in being assertive; it is quite a valued skill both in a person's personal life and in their work or professional life.

Assertiveness Is a Skill, Not a Personality Trait

Assertiveness, communication, conflict resolution, confidence, and leadership. What do all of these have in common? All of these are skills and not innate characteristics. What does this mean? I will start by defining these two terms for you. A learned skill, as I am sure you can imagine, is something that you can learn and develop in order to possess. This is the opposite of an innate characteristic, which is something that you are born with. For instance, the color of your eyes or certain aspects of your personality, such as being stubborn.

Skills are things that you can study, practice, and improve upon. Skills are things like communication or cooking. On the other hand, a characteristic is something that you possess that you do not have much control over. You can work on things like becoming less stubborn, but for the most part, you are born a stubborn person, or you are not.

Remember, in the introduction to this book when we discussed the differences between a *fixed mindset* and a *growth mindset*? This comes into play here once again, as you must check your mindset before setting out to make changes. Having a fixed mindset makes a person highly concerned with what skills and intelligence they currently have, and those that they were born with, and it does not allow them any room to focus on what they can develop or improve upon. Therefore, their activities are limited to the capacity that they think they have.

However, those with growth mindsets understand that skills and intelligence are something that can be developed and learned throughout the course of their life. This can be done through reading, education, training, mentorships, or simply just passion. They understand that their brain is a muscle that can be 'worked out' to grow stronger. Knowing this, you must employ a growth mindset. Every single skill you have, as well as your intelligence and confidence, can be improved or changed by putting in the effort to do so. Famous public figures of success like Oprah Winfrey, Steve Jobs, and Bill Gates all employed a growth mindset, which allowed them to overcome every obstacle that got in their way. Rather than succumbing to defeat, they worked and discovered innovative ways to overcome previous failures and found success at the end.

Think about what mindset you have right now. If you

142

already have a growth mindset, you simply need to continue practicing it while being proactive about dealing with obstacles and overcoming failures. If you think you are someone with a fixed mindset, you must change it right now. Believe me when I tell you that confidence and skills such as assertiveness can be improved upon with time and hard work, and this book will show you how. If you don't believe me, just try it. Pick a random skill; this could be knitting, computer programming, jogging, or anything that can be learned. Set goals for yourself and begin learning something new. If you can take something that you have zero skill in and become proficient in it, you have just proved to yourself that growth mindsets are real and fixed mindsets only hold you back from success. This is proof that the only thing holding you back from becoming a more assertive and confident you, is your mindset.

Take some time to consider this and evaluate yourself and your mindset before moving on, as it will play a vital part in your success throughout this book and life.

The Benefits of Assertiveness

There are numerous benefits to assertiveness, many of which you are likely aware of, or you would not have opened this book in the first place. In this section, we will look at some of the most valuable benefits of being an assertive person.

- Being assertive allows you to communicate in a confident and clear way
- Being assertive allows you to practice self-care by setting boundaries and sticking to them
- Being assertive allows you to deal with conflict in your personal and professional lives most effectively and maturely possible
- Being assertive allows you to share your ideas and thoughts persuasively and calmly, which will command attention and respect
- Being assertive allows you to ensure your needs are being met
- Being assertive allows you to feel comfortable and confident, saying "no."
- Being assertive helps you to provide feedback to others in a constructive and effective way

- Being assertive improves your interpersonal skills
- Being assertive helps you to be more confident in yourself and your decisions and ideas
- Being assertive helps you to reduce your stress levels by helping you to confidently prioritize your time and energy
- Being assertive increases your self-respect, self-confidence, and self-worth
- Being assertive helps you to be a better negotiator
- Being assertive helps you to remain calm under pressure

Why Many People Struggle With Assertiveness

One of the main reasons that people struggle with being assertive is because it is a means to protect oneself. A person may not even realize that they are doing this to protect themselves, and they may genuinely want to be more assertive. Still, many people have trouble with this because the avoidance of being assertive helps a person feel as though they are in control of their life by avoiding the possibility of negative emotions. This is what is called a defensive measure. Defensive measures are actions that a person takes to avoid getting hurt or to minimize the risk of getting hurt. External defensive behaviors are a type of defensive measure that is used to help a person prevent harm or conflict with other people. This includes being non-assertive, being submissive, silencing yourself, blaming yourself, and keeping distance between yourself and others. This is a common reason that people have a lack of assertiveness, and it is something that we will address heavily in this book.

Behind this effort to avoid getting hurt, there could be many reasons. The most common reasons begin in childhood, believe it or not. Our upbringing and childhood experiences typically play a massive role in your level of self-esteem in your adult life. Did you grow up in a strict family who barely ever gave you praise? Did a more successful sibling always overshadow you? Did you grow up in a family where nobody was ever around, and you were left to fend for yourself? These are all examples and reasons why people may have lower self-esteem compared to others. Studies show that children who were raised in families or households where love was not often shown or expressed, typically had lower levels of self-esteem later in life when compared to children that were shown love or who grew up in families where love was expressed.

Further, in an incredibly fast-paced society with the obsessive usage of social media, it is so difficult not to compare ourselves to others. Have you ever found yourself obsessively stalking or following a celebrity's Instagram page? Are you continually following people who became millionaires at the ripe age of 22? Or are you following gorgeous models who have the world's population fiending for them? In this day and age, our exposure to hotter, wealthier, and more successful people are continuously growing. Seeing incredible success like this every day really makes it hard for you to recognize your self-worth and, in turn, lowers your self-esteem.

How Assertiveness Is Linked to Self-Esteem

When people have a healthy level of self-esteem, they typically have a positive outlook on themselves. They believe in their capabilities to achieve goals and do not spend a lot of time dwelling on failure. They are not afraid to ask for help from others to help them reach their goals. They are also able to be assertive and be able to say "no" to situations or requests that they do not want to do.

Having a healthy level of self-esteem helps increase assertiveness because you believe in what you are saying and doing. If you believe that you need or want something, you won't spend time dwelling on whether you think other people think it is true, you will just ask for it. Those who have low self-esteem typically suffer from not being able to ask for what they need or want because they are afraid of being judged or rejected. In their minds, asking for something for 'need' is a sign of weakness, and therefore, people will judge them for asking for it. On the flip side, somebody with a healthy level of self-esteem typically isn't afraid of that because that hasn't even crossed their mind. Since having

148

healthy self-esteem comes from loving yourself and respecting yourself, it feels perfectly reasonable to ask for what they feel like they need and want.

For this reason, self-esteem and assertiveness are inextricably linked, and to work on one, we must work on the other. Throughout this book, you will see how self-esteem and assertiveness play into one another and how they come together in many different situations.

To help you understand further what being assertive means, I will provide you with an example. Imagine if your mother wanted you to come over to her house as soon as possible so you can help her pack up her things to prepare for a move. However, you had planned to spend your evening relaxing, watching a movie, and taking a hot bubble bath because you have had a busy week at work. Assertiveness, in this case, would be valuing your own needs just as much as you value your mother's needs. A person with a healthy amount of self-esteem will be able to demonstrate assertiveness by saying, "I am worthy of this. I deserve my break when I need it." Somebody with low self-esteem will typically think, "It will be selfish of me to take a break when somebody needs my help." A part of having self-esteem is being able to understand that you can't pour from an empty glass. In the example above, those with low self-esteem will go and help their mother move anyway despite being exhausted and end up feeling like other people do not respect their time and feelings. In reality, people do not know what you need if you are unable to communicate it. In the next chapter, we are going to look at communication styles and the most effective styles for being assertive and expressing yourself clearly.

Communication Styles

When it comes to being more assertive, understanding communication is essential. In this chapter, we are going to look at communication and how to be an effective communicator. Once you learn this, it will be much easier to work on improving your assertiveness, which is why we are addressing communication so early on in this book. We will begin by looking at what communication is, in its most basic form, and then we will look at different communication styles and when they are most useful.

What Is Communication?

Communication, in its most basic form, is a way of exchanging information with others. There are many ways that we can communicate with others, including verbal and nonverbal methods. In addition, with the advent of technology, a plethora of additional means of communication have been created.

Communication is not only an essential part of our relationships but also our day-to-day life in general. You will often communicate with people in some way without even having a relationship with them. For example, when you go to the store, you will communicate with the cashier. You may also give a nod or a look to someone else in their car as a form of communication. Communication is essential when living in a society of humans and is even present among other species. Communication has been key to interpersonal connections long before the modern languages we know and use now came about. Being able to communicate effectively is useful for interactions in your workplace, in your home and family life, in your leisure activities, and in your everyday interactions as you move through the world alongside other people.

Everybody has the ability to use basic communication- this propensity for verbal communication is something that humans are born with, which is why we are able to learn languages with such ease as babies. This does not mean, however, that everybody can communicate effectively or with skill. The most basic level of communication involves things like being able to speak simple words and phrases and being able to recognize and tell someone what your basic needs are (such as being hungry or having to go to the bathroom). Basic communication also includes being able to hear what another person is saying to you and understanding what it means at a surface level.

Verbal Communication

Verbal or oral communication uses spoken words to communicate a message. Within verbal communication, there are different types. We are going to look at these types in more detail.

Intrapersonal communication is a type of communication that only involves oneself. This can also be referred to as "silent conversations with ourselves." It comes in the form of thoughts and ideas and goes on within your mind consciously or subconsciously. We use this type of communication, while making decisions about our actions or thinking about concepts. We will often switch back and forth between the listener and the speaker during this type of communication as we are, in a way, bouncing ideas off of ourselves. This type of communication can remain intrapersonal if not shared with others, or it can become the next type of communication that we will look at if we then decide to verbalize it with others.

This next form of verbal communication is called Interpersonal communication. While the words intrapersonal and interpersonal seem similar at first glance, their meaning is different. Interpersonal communication means communication between two people. This typically occurs with two individuals having a one-on-one interaction. In this type of communication both persons are the listener and the speaker, and they will switch back and forth between roles depending on who is speaking.

Nonverbal Communication

Communication can be taken much further than the basics, as there are many small and subtle ways that people communicate their thoughts and feelings without saying a word. Being able to pick up on these types of communications while interacting with someone is what sets basic communication apart from effective and intelligent communication.

This type of communication is called nonverbal communication.

Nonverbal communication influences a large percentage of what humans base their first impressions of others on. Because of this, it is essential to understand what the things we see are telling us about another person, and what we may be telling others through our own body language.

First, though, what exactly do we mean when we say nonverbal communication? This term includes a wide variety of ways that people communicate without using words. This involves things that people do (or do not do) that send messages about what they think and feel. Humans are quite selective about what they choose to share with others. They choose when and whom to share information with, but their bodies sometimes tell a different story. This type of physical, bodily communication can be either a conscious or unconscious action, meaning that we may not even be aware that we are sharing our thoughts, feelings, or opinions in ways other than through our words. It is essential to understand this concept because of what messages you may be sending and also what others may be saying without being aware of it.

One example of nonverbal communication is the use of vocal dynamics. Vocal communication may seem similar to verbal communication; however, there is a lot more to a sentence than the words it contains. The way that someone delivers a sentence is much more telling than the words it contains. For example, the inclusion of a pause or a drawn-out word and even complete silence can tell you about a person's internal state. If a person becomes suddenly silent, they may be offended by the topic of conversation or by something that was said. If the person avoids silence at all costs, they are likely a nervous or anxious person who is uncomfortable with a silent moment or two. The tone of voice and volume play a critical part in this as well.

If you didn't understand a word that someone was saying but could read their nonverbal communication cues, you would be able to tell a lot about what they were trying to convey. Like facial expressions, this is another type of nonverbal communication that we learn when we are very young. We can tell the difference between a happy and an angry sentence even before we have a full vocabulary to use and understand the meaning of the sentence. The volume of a person's voice can also indicate traits of their personality or their current state. If they are speaking very quietly, they are probably shy or nervous, while a loud volume can mean that they are angry or excited. A great example of the tone of a person's voice demonstrating more than what their words are saying is sarcasm. When we are using sarcasm, the tone of our

156

voice is precisely the opposite of what we are saying.

The message we are trying to convey is not evident in the words we are saying, but rather the tone in which we are saying them. If someone were to misunderstand our tone, they could become perplexed as to what we meant. If we say, "I loved waiting in line for four hours," the tone we say it with indicates that we actually mean exactly the opposite. By choosing the appropriate vocal dynamics, you can convey assertiveness.

Body Language

Body language is a fairly broad term and can include a variety of different forms of nonverbal communication, such as hand gestures and facial expressions, but also includes things like touch and head movements.

Body language can be conscious or unconscious. Most of us are very familiar with conscious body language as we more than likely use this as a form of communication on a regular basis.

An example of a deliberate display of body language would be the use of hand signals. These vary between cultures and regions of the world, but every culture has some. They may change with changes in pop culture, or they may be long-standing such as the thumbs up in North America. These hand signals are a form of body language that we use to convey specific messages to others.

Another example is a handshake. A handshake is a nonverbal way of saying that you are welcoming someone to make contact with you and is a friendly greeting upon meeting someone new.

Another example of conscious body language is facial expressions. There are many facial expressions that we consciously make to convey messages to people. Facial expressions can express anger, sadness, or happiness. Humans often make these facial expressions to tell others how they feel without speaking. Have you ever been with your partner in a situation where they said something that frustrated you, and you gave them a specific look to let them know that they have upset you? With this one simple facial expression, they know what you are thinking and feeling.

We will now look at unconscious body language in terms of different areas of the body. We will examine all of these different areas and what they may be telling us by their actions. The face is where we will begin. The face is very involved when it comes to deciphering nonverbal communication because it has so much to tell us. There are many different places to look for clues on the face.

The Eyes

Firstly, the eyes. Our eyes operate significantly on their own accord- blinking when they need to and gazing where there is movement. While we can most often control where they look, they will sometimes operate on their own in interactions with others. The eyes will often be the first place to show how the person is feeling. Our brain and our spinal cord make up the pairing that is known as the central nervous system. This pathway of neurons operates fully automatically- that is to say, with no help from our conscious mind. The eyes are connected to this nervous system and are the only part of the system that faces the outside of the body. Because of this, the eyes are intertwined with what we are thinking and feeling, even more than we notice. The brain and the spinal cord give us life- they are responsible for initiating our movements, our thoughts, and our feelings. "The eyes are the window to the soul" got its origins in this fact of anatomy. It is very difficult to control the emotions and sentiments that people can see in our eyes as they come directly from the places within us over which we have no control. The eyes, therefore, are the first place to look when it comes to seeing someone's truth.

Eye contact is a significant indicator of the intentions of a person. As previously discussed, the amount of eye contact someone is making is an indicator of their level of comfort. If someone is making and holding eye contact for an extended period of time without looking away, they appear to be very comfortable to the point of seeming like they may have predetermined intentions. If someone is avoiding eye contact altogether, they tend to seem very untrustworthy, almost as if they are trying very hard to hide something from you. We have all encountered an uncomfortable amount of eye contact, whether too much or too little, where it made us feel like something was not right. You may have been feeling unease but were unaware as to why. Feeling someone's eyes staring directly into yours with no end in sight makes for a lot of discomfort, while trying to catch someone's eye who is clearly making an effort to avoid yours makes for a very awkward conversation. If someone is making steady eye contact, looking away now and then, and then coming back to meet your eyes once again, they are probably feeling comfortable in the situation or conversation and are quite secure with themselves and their position. This amount of eye contact makes us feel comfortable in the other person's presence and think that their intentions are pure.

The Arms

The arms themselves can close us off or open us up to the world. The positioning of the arms in relation to the body can be something that happens automatically. Someone may be extremely comfortable with the situation they are in if they have their arms at their sides, or resting on the armrests of the chair in which they are seated. This may happen automatically as a result of feeling unthreatened and safe in their surroundings.

Arms behind the back indicate that the person is feeling secure and welcoming a challenge. We know this because they have their protecting elements (their arms) behind them and their chest out and exposed, meaning that they will not be able to quickly protect themselves if need be. This is an indication of feeling secure and comfortable or feeling like they are stronger than those around them.

There are even more places to look for body language cues, some of which we will examine in more detail later on in this book when we look at how to read a person and how you can exhibit assertive body language.

The 4 Communication Styles

As you now know, communication comes in many different forms, but in this case, we are going to look at different styles of verbal communication. There are four styles of verbal communication that we will examine. They are as follows.

Aggressive Communication Style

The first communication style we will explore is the Aggressive Communication Style. This communication style is borne out of a place of fear. This person fears they will not be heard or understood, and therefore, they enter into interaction or conversation with a loud volume and an attitude of entitlement. They approach the conversation with a wide stance and a confrontational posture. They feel the need to shout over others and force their point of view. This style of communication can often end up having the exact effect the communicator is trying to avoid, which is that people may not end up listening to the content of the sentences because they are distracted by the way that it has been conveyed. When people are faced with an aggressive communication style, they tend to become defensive and closed-off, unwilling to engage much further in the interaction.

Passive Communication Style

163

The second is the Passive Communication Style. This type of communicator prefers to avoid conflict at all costs. They would rather please people than to make their opinion known. They are easily swayed, and they tend to speak with a very low volume. They attempt to shrink themselves down using their body language with hunched shoulders and crossed arms. They feel as if their opinions are not valid and are apologetic if they think that someone disagrees with them. Other people will approach this type of communicator in an exasperated manner as they feel that they have to walk on eggshells in an effort to preserve the person's feelings.

Passive-Aggressive Communication Style

The next is the Passive-Aggressive Communication Style. These types of communicators initially show one type of attitude on the outside, that their words do not match. They use passive, self-shrinking body language, therefore, appearing to be submissive and non-confrontational on the outside, while communicating with their words in an aggressive manner. It is the combination of both of the previous two styles of communication. They tend to speak aggressively to indirectly make a point but act out passively in front of the person. Their words are of an aggressive nature, but they deliver them in a passive style. They will use a low volume and a gentle tone while saying something likely to cause confrontation or to make someone angry. People tend to become frustrated when dealing with this type of communicator because there is a lot of close attention that needs to be paid to figure out what exactly they are trying to say. It is often used by people who wish to be of an aggressive style but who are afraid to speak out in such a way.

Assertive Communication Style

The final verbal communication style is the Assertive Communication Style. This style of communication is rooted in confidence and self-assuredness. People who communicate in this way have confident body language and maintain eye contact; they are relaxed but engaged. They are emphatic but maintain a normal volume and tone of voice. They are secure in their stance both literally and figuratively and are unafraid of rejection or a disagreeing party. They communicate

165

their points with a calm but firm demeanor.

This type of communicator is the easiest to communicate with as they are able to remain level-headed in disagreement and are not forceful in any way. They are not trying to enforce an attitude of superiority, nor are they trying to stay hidden. They stand in interaction as they are and are not trying too hard to be anything that they are not. People respect the fact that this communicator is able to speak their truth concisely and directly without being aggressive.

Outcomes of the 4 Communication Styles

Each of these different communication styles will result in a different outcome. It is essential to understand these outcomes so that you can choose your method of communication wisely and so that you can see how some of these communication styles are less desirable. We will begin by looking at the outcomes of each of the four communication styles.

Aggressive Communication Style: I win you lose

Passive Communication Style: I lose you win

Passive Aggressive Communication Style: I lose you lose

Assertive Communication Style: I win you win

As you can see, each of these styles results in a different outcome, and with each outcome, specific feelings, and takeaways for each person. From this, you can see why the assertive communication style is the best choice and why in this book, we are focused on using this communication style in almost every scenario and encounter that you will find yourself in.

For example, if someone approaches you with an aggressive communication style, you can glean that they do not have much interest in what you may have to contribute to the discussion and maybe quite forceful with their words.

167

They are interested in "winning" themselves and are intent on having you "lose." Knowing the different styles and how to recognize them can help you to avoid being offended and hurt if someone approaches you in this way and can also help you to determine how to respond appropriately.

How To Use Different Communication Styles In Different Situations

Some of these communication styles may be more effective than others in different situations. There may be some situations where communicating more passively is required, and some situations in which a more balanced, assertive style is the best choice.

Being aware of the different styles and how they sound and look (in terms of body language) can help you to choose which one to use and when depending on the situation and with whom you are interacting. All of these communication styles come with their own characteristic body language, which can help you to identify them. Understanding this can help you to determine which style is being used when communicating with others, as well as which styles others are using to communicate with you.

How to Be Aware of Your Own Communication Style

We may all exhibit a combination of all of these styles but can usually pin ourselves down to one style the majority of the time. Understanding this about ourselves will aid us in communicating our thoughts and ideas more effectively but will also help us in being better able to receive and understand the communication of others' feelings and ideas. Being honest with ourselves and recognizing which style we use the most can help us to analyze our interactions and see why people may react to us in one way or another. Awareness is the key to changing anything, and choosing the most effective communication style will allow you to see other people's true personalities instead of seeing their reaction to your choice of communication style.

To examine your communication style, it is best to examine your body language, your tone of voice, and your choice of words. It is also important to examine how all of these are working together as a whole. By doing this, you will be able to determine your communication style and then decide whether it is effective or if you should work on changing this.

Get your full copy today! *__The Keys to Being Brilliantly Confident and More Assertive: A Vital Guide to Enhancing Your Communication Skills, Getting Rid of Anxiety, and Building Assertiveness.__*"

BOOKS BY RICHARD BANKS

How to be Charismatic, Develop Confidence, and
Exude Leadership: The Miracle Formula for Magnetic
Charisma, Defeating Anxiety, and Winning at
Communication

How to Stop Being Negative, Angry, and Mean:
Master Your Mind and Take Control of Your Life

How to Deal with Grief, Loss, and Death: A Survivor's
Guide to Coping with Pain and Trauma, and Learning
to Live Again

How to Deal With Stress, Depression, and Anxiety: A
Vital Guide on How to Deal with Nerves and Coping
with Stress, Pain, OCD and Trauma

The Positive Guide to Anger Management: The Most
Practical Guide on How to Be Calmer, Learn to Defeat
Anger, Deal with Angry People, and Living a Life of

Mental Wellness and Positivity

Develop a Positive Mindset and Attract the Life of Your Dreams: Unleash Positive Thinking to Achieve Unbound Happiness, Health, and Success

The Keys to Being Brilliantly Confident and More Assertive: A Vital Guide to Enhancing Your Communication Skills, Getting Rid of Anxiety, and Building Assertiveness

Personal Development Mastery 2 Books in 1: The Keys to being Brilliantly Confident and More Assertive + How to be Charismatic, Develop Confidence, and Exude Leadership

Positive Mindset Mastery 2 Books in 1: Develop a Positive Mindset and Attract the Life of Your Dreams + How to Stop Being Negative, Angry, and Mean